Janie's Vegan

COOKBOOK

First published edition 2020

UK Book Publishing Group
First Floor Unit 5,
305, Whitley Road
Whitley Bay
Tyne & Wear
NE26 2HU

ISBN: 978-1-913179-93-9

Janie's Vegan COOKBOOK

Written by

Jane L Tate

PREFACE

It all started around the age of six. I distinctly remember that particular Sunday lunch-time and continuously chewing that roast beef, which I could only compare with what I would imagine to be like chewing the sole of my shoe. I gagged on it and from that day I refused to eat meat. At the time I didn't relate eating meat to the killing of animals.

From that point I grew up as a pescatarian, the same as my Mum. On the odd occasion I did eat fish, but most of the time I was a vegetarian and a very, very fussy one. My total diet consisted of baked beans, fish fingers, cheese, eggs, (but only the yolk), chips or any form of potato.

At 16 years old I left home, moved abroad and continued to be just as fussy. That was when I learnt to cook, discovering I had the ability to cook great meals without ever tasting them. Eventually I had three wonderful children and I decided very early on that I didn't want them as fussy as me. When they reached the age of questioning why they were eating different food to me, I replied that I was grown up and they were still growing.

At 38 years of age I was fortunate to go to New Zealand which involved a long flight of 24 hours. Unfortunately, there were no chips or baked beans on the flight and I became increasingly very hungry. That was the first time in my life that I tasted rice, asparagus, broccoli and carrots. It was quite scary to try these new foods, but it opened up a whole new, amazing world to me. I met my friend in New Zealand and we went to lots of different restaurants, even having pasta for the first time. That flight changed my life forever!

By the end of 2016 I was unwell, which was another turning point in my life. I have a friend who was unwell 10 years ago who was told he was a "walking dead man." He changed to a Vegan diet and I am very happy to say he is still alive today. I think we all recognise that what we consume must affect our health, together with other influences. I therefore also decided to change to a fully Vegan diet.

Some may say I am not a true Vegan in the sense that some of my possessions are made from leather. These, however, were acquired prior to changing my diet. I try to be eco-friendly, so I shall use them until they are worn out. My diet, however, is definitely Vegan and I feel a whole lot better for it. Most importantly, I've been given the all clear with the illness.

By eating Vegan, we help ourselves and all those beautiful animals, that have as much right to live as we do.

I decided to write this book because I wanted to share my own recipes with others. I find it very confusing to follow recipes myself and it's been a very difficult task to write this book. I am mildly dyslexic and I get muddled quite easily. My natural way of cooking is to just throw it all in. I never normally weigh anything. You may therefore imagine how difficult it has been. To make things easier, I have made some of the recipes with QR codes, so you can watch how to do it along with the recipe. Although I am not a great photographer, I can assure you that it all tastes delicious!

I would like to thank all my family and friends for their support and patience whilst writing this book and for being the chief tasters.

Happy Cooking.

MEASUREMENTS AND ABBREVIATIONS

tsp = teaspoon

dsp = dessert spoon

tbsp = tablespoon

ml = millilitres

l or L = litre

g = grams

kg = kilogram

°C = degrees Celsius

I use a fan oven for my recipes, unless otherwise stated. If you use a conventional oven then you may need to increase the temperature slightly or cook a little longer.

ALL ingredients are vegan even when not specified in my recipes. Not all labelling mentions vegan but if you check through the ingredients and there are no dairy or animal products then I do still use them.

Always check recommendations when using your own appliances.

I don't generally like to waste any food so I normally use any leftover vegetables to make soups, just cook and blend.

Left over fruits usually get blended into smoothies.

The egg replacers which I use are as follows: I drain a tin of chickpeas and whisk the liquid until stiff. Or I use a bought one called Orgran.

I use various different stock. I sometimes use the leftover water from boiling vegetables or stock cubes, or stock powder.

The main stock powder I use is made by a company called Osem. It's called Chicken Flavour soup and seasoning mix. This stock liquid is Parve, which means it has no meat or dairy products in it. I have contacted the company and they assure me there is also no fish products either. Great flavoured stock.

CONTENTS

SOUPS & STARTERS

Asparagus & Mushroom Soup 2
Broccoli & Cheese Soup 4
Carrot & Coriander Soup 6
Cream of Cashew & Vegetable Soup 8
Potato & Kale Soup 10
Potato & Leek Comfort Soup 12
Pumpkin Soup 14
Squash & Noodle Soup 16
Sweet Potato Soup 18
Tomato & Quinoa Soup 20
Spicy Aubergine Salsa Salad 22
Hummus & Tahini dip 24
Lentil Salad 26
Mushroom Appetiser 28
Nutritious Organic Salad 30
Potato Bourekas 32
Quinoa Salad 34
Simple Salad Middle Eastern Style 36

MAINS

Stuffed Aubergine 40
Chickpea & Sweet Potato Burger cakes 42
Black Bean Chilli 44
Vegan Mince Chilli 46
Moroccan Style Cous-Cous 48
Falafel 50
Potato Gnocchi 52
Vegan Lasagne 54
Spaghetti & Spicy Meatballs 56

Creamy Vegetable Medley 58
Moussaka 60
Mushroom Stack 62
Mini Nut Loaf 64
Mince Parcel 66
Nutty Parcel 68
Steamed Pak Choi with trimmings 70
Mince & Wild Mushroom Pie 72
Artichoke & Olive Pizza 74
Pizza Base 76
Green Quiche 78
Spinach Ravioli 80
Spicy Rice & Lentils 82
Spicy Rice & Vegetables 84
Rice & Tofu 86
Pumpkin & Pea Risotto 88
Meaty Vegan Sausages 90
Vegan Shakshuka 92
Shepherd's Pie 94
Quick Spaghetti 96
Hamin (slow cooker Stew) 98
Vegan Meatball Stew 100
Mushroom Stroganoff 102
Cheesy Open Tart 104

DESSERTS

Bread & Butter Pudding 108
Chocolate Button Buns 110
Chocolate Chip Cookies 112
Chocolate & Coconut Mousse 114
Chocolate Orange Cake 116
Chocolate Orange Cookies 118
Coconut Cookies 120
Date filled Cookies 122

Homemade Cereal   124
Homemade Protein Bars   126
Lemon Cheesecake   128
Lime Cheesecake   130
Strawberry Cheesecake   132
Rhubarb Crumble Pie   134
Basic Sponge cake   136
Milky Cake   138
Vegan Tiramisu   140

DRINKS, SMOOTHIES & MISCELLANEOUS

Blackberry Smoothie   144
Blueberry Smoothie   145
Detox Drink   146
Energy Smoothie   147
Green Tea & Pineapple Drink   148
Hazelnut Milk Smoothie   149
Caramelised Onions   150
Homemade Pasta Sauce   151
Quick Pasta Sauce   152
Sweet Potato Mash   153
Granary Rolls   154
Olive Flat Bread   156

# Starters

ASPARAGUS & MUSHROOM SOUP

PREPARATION

Preparation: 10 minutes

Total Cooking Time: 35 minutes

Serves: 4 – 6 helpings

Oven: 0

NUTRITIONAL INFORMATION

ASPARAGUS

Low calorie vegetable, packed with Vitamin A, C & K and many other nutrients

TOP TIPS

If your asparagus is getting a little old (woody) then cut them in very small rings and they will taste just as good and nothing is wasted.

INGREDIENTS

200g Asparagus

100g Chestnut Mushrooms

2 L Vegetable Stock

200g baby Potatoes

2 small Celery stalks

½ red Bell Pepper

1 Carrot

½ tsp of Cumin

½ tsp Turmeric

1 tsp Harissa

1 tbsp Tomato Purée

½ tsp Mustard

METHOD

Roughly chop the asparagus, leaving the tips whole

Wash the mushrooms and cut in halves

Chop the celery into small pieces

Wash and slice the carrot, discarding the top and tail

Combine all ingredients into a large saucepan

Bring to the boil, then lower the heat and simmer for 30 minutes

BROCCOLI & CHEESE SOUP

PREPARATION

Preparation: 10 minutes

Total Cooking Time: 33 minutes

Serves: 4 helpings

Oven: 0

NUTRITIONAL INFORMATION

BROCCOLI

Good source of vitamin K and Calcium

TOP TIPS

Best served hot with crispy bread and spread with vegan hard block butter

INGREDIENTS

300g Broccoli florets

1.5L Vegetable Stock

2 crushed Garlic Cloves

60g Coconut Collaborate

120g thick creamy Cheese (violife)

Handful of Spinach

3 tbsp Corn Flour or Pea Protein

1 tbsp Oil

¼ tsp Paprika

METHOD

Peel and crush the garlic with the back of a metal spoon

Heat the oil in a saucepan

Gently fry the garlic in the oil for 3 minutes

Add the stock and corn flour to the garlic and bring to the boil

Stir well

Add all remaining ingredients

Simmer for 30 minutes

CARROT & CORIANDER SOUP

PREPARATION

Preparation: 10 minutes

Cooking Time: 20 minutes on hob

Serves: 4 helpings

Oven: 0

NUTRITIONAL INFORMATION
CARROTS

High in Vitamin A

TOP TIPS

Best served hot with crispy bread

INGREDIENTS

6 medium Carrots

1.5 L Vegetable Stock

30g flat leaf Coriander

2 tbsp Gram Flour (chickpea flour)

100ml single Soya Cream

1 tbsp Coconut Oil

1 tsp Harissa

1 tsp English Mustard

¼ tsp each of Cumin, Turmeric and Paprika

METHOD

Wash and roughly chop the carrots into small chunks

Combine all ingredients into a large saucepan.

Cook for 20 minutes

Once cooked, use a hand held blender and blend the soup

Take care not to splash the hot soup over yourself.

CREAM OF CASHEW & VEGETABLE SOUP

PREPARATION

Preparation: 20 minutes

Cooking Time: 30 minutes on hob
Or all day in the slow cooker

Serves: 6

Oven: 0

NUTRITIONAL INFORMATION

CASHEW NUTS

They have a lower fat content than most nuts and contain monounsaturated fats.
Also contain, magnesium, iron, protein Potassium and Vitamin B-6

TOP TIPS

Best served hot with crispy bread
This is one of my favorite soups

INGREDIENTS

400g Potatoes
150g Cashew Nuts puréed
200g Sweet Potatoes
200g Carrots
80g tinned Sweetcorn
1 medium Red Onion
2 cloves of Garlic
1 Celery stalk
Handful of Spinach
1 red Pepper
1.5 L Stock
2 sprigs of fresh Dill
1tsp mixed Herbs
5g fresh chopped Chives
¼ tsp dried crushed Chili

METHOD

Peel & chop the potatoes, sweet potatoes and carrots into small cubes

Peel & chop the onions and garlic into small pieces

Chop the celery and pepper into small pieces

Fry the onions, garlic, pepper and celery in the oil for 5 minutes

Use a little of the liquid from the stock to purée the cashew in a blender

Combine all ingredients into a large saucepan

Cook for 30 minutes and serve hot

Or you could place in a slow cooker on low heat and leave all day.

Always check the recommendations on your slow cooker

POTATO & KALE SOUP

PREPARATION

Preparation: 10 minutes

Cooking Time: 30 minutes

Serves: 4 -6 helpings

Oven: 0

NUTRITIONAL INFORMATION

KALE

Good source of Vitamin A, C & K contains Protein, fibre and antioxidants

TOP TIPS

Best served hot with crispy bread and spread with vegan hard block butter

INGREDIENTS

4 small Potatoes

2 small Sweet Potatoes

1 small Squash

2 handfuls of Kale

1 tbsp Rapeseed Oil

1.5 L Vegetable Stock

½ tsp Chili Flakes

½ tsp Turmeric

½ tsp Cumin

METHOD

Peel all the potatoes and chop roughly

Peel and de-seed the squash and also chop roughly

Bring the stock to the boil and add all ingredients to the stock

Simmer for 30 minutes

When vegetables are tender, use a potato masher and gently mash them in the saucepan.

Serve hot with homemade bread.

POTATO & LEEK SOUP

PREPARATION

Preparation: 10 minutes

Cooking Time: 30 minutes

Total Time: 40 minutes

Serves: 4

Oven: 0

NUTRITIONAL INFORMATION

LEEKS

Low in cholesterol, low in fat and a good source of Vitamin A & C

TOP TIPS

Best served hot with crispy bread and spread with vegan hard block butter

INGREDIENTS

500g peeled Potatoes

200g sliced Leeks

1L Chicken flavor OSEM Stock

½ tsp hot Paprika

¼ tsp Turmeric

1 tbsp Rapeseed Oil

1 tin of Chickpeas puréed with their own liquid

Sprig of fresh Thyme chopped

Black Pepper to taste

METHOD

Heat the stock

Heat the oil in a separate pan

Fry the sliced leeks in the oil for 5 minutes

Peel and chop the potatoes into small cubes

Place all ingredients into the stock and simmer for 25 minutes

PUMPKIN SOUP

PREPARATION

Preparation: 10 minutes

Cooking Time: 30 minutes on hob
Or all day in the slow cooker

Serves: 4 helpings

Oven: 0

NUTRITIONAL INFORMATION

PUMPKIN

Low in saturated fat and very low in cholesterol. Contains many vitamins

TOP TIPS

You can wash the seeds, dry them and then roast in the oven with salt. Delicious healthy snack and nothing goes to waste.

INGREDIENTS

1 small Pumpkin

3 cloves Garlic

1.5L Vegetable Stock

1 tbsp Rapeseed Oil

½ tsp mixed Herbs

½ tsp crushed Black Pepper

METHOD

Peel and de-seed the pumpkin

Chop into bite size cubes

Peel the garlic

Combine all ingredients into a saucepan and bring to the boil.

Simmer for 30 minutes.

When cooked, use a hand held blender to liquidize, be careful not to splash yourself. This makes the soup thicker.

If you prefer your soup much thicker, you can add a tablespoon of corn flour, then liquidize.

SQUASH & NOODLE SOUP

PREPARATION

Preparation: 10 minutes

Cooking Time: 25 minutes

Total Time: 35 minutes

Serves: 4

Oven: 0

NUTRITIONAL INFORMATION

BUTTERNUT SQUASH

Good source of Vitamin E and Potassium

TOP TIPS

Best served hot with crispy bread and spread with vegan hard block butter

INGREDIENTS

1 medium Butternut Squash

1.5 L Vegetable Stock

2 cloves of Garlic crushed

45g whole grain dry Rice Noodles (vermicelli, very thin rice noodles)

15g fresh Basil

½ tsp Paprika

½ tsp Turmeric

½ tsp Cumin

Black Pepper to taste

METHOD

Heat the stock together with all the herbs and spices

Peel the squash and garlic (crush the garlic)

Chop the squash into 1cm cubes

Place the squash and garlic into the stock and simmer for 20 minutes

After 20 minutes use a hand held electric blender and liquidize the

soup. Be careful not to splash yourself.

Crush the rice noodles in your hand and add them to the soup

Continue to cook for a further 5 minutes.

SWEET POTATO SOUP

PREPARATION

Preparation: 10 minutes

Cooking Time: 30 minutes on hob

Serves: 4 helpings

Oven: 0

NUTRITIONAL INFORMATION

SWEET POTATOES

High in Vitamin A, No cholesterol and no saturated fats

TOP TIPS

Best served hot with crispy bread

INGREDIENTS

2 medium Sweet Potatoes

2 medium Parsnips

1.5 L Vegetable Stock

1 red Onion

1 red bell Pepper

1 clove of Garlic

Large handful of Spinach

1 tbsp Gram Flour

1 tbsp Oil

½ L boiling Water

METHOD

Peel and chop the sweet potatoes and parsnips into small pieces

Cook them in the stock for 25 minutes

Chop the onion, pepper and garlic

Fry the chopped onion, pepper and garlic in the oil until tender

In a separate bowl, place the gram flour and boiling water, mix well

Remove the sweet potatoes and parsnips from the hob

Use a hand held blender to liquidize them, then place back on the hob

Place all ingredients into the liquidized mixture and cook for a further 5 minutes.

Add salt and pepper if required

TOMATO & QUINOA SOUP

PREPARATION

Preparation: 10 minutes

Cooking Time: 20 minutes on hob

Serves: 4 helpings

Oven: 0

NUTRITIONAL INFORMATION

TOMATOES

Good source of Antioxidant Lycopene and Vitamin C & K

TOP TIPS

Best served hot with homemade bread

INGREDIENTS

800g fresh Tomatoes
4 cloves of Garlic
4 sprigs of fresh Basil
100g Quinoa
1.5 L Stock
1 tbsp Tomato Purèe
½ tsp Chilli Flakes

METHOD

Heat the stock in a large saucepan
Add the chilli flakes and quinoa to the stock
Wash the tomatoes
Peel the garlic
Place the tomatoes, garlic, basil and purèe in a blender, blend for 10 seconds.
Pour the tomato liquid into the stock.
Simmer for 15 minutes

SPICY AUBERGINE SALSA SALAD

PREPARATION

Preparation: 10 minutes
Plus 30 minutes soaking

Cooking Time: 40 minutes

Serves: 4

Oven: 0

NUTRITIONAL INFORMATION

AUBERGINE

Good source of Dietary Fibre
Vitamin B1, B6 and Potassium

TOP TIPS

This can be eaten hot but it is better cold. Leave to cool in the fridge. Tastes even better if left for the next day. Great served with pitta bread and hummus.

INGREDIENTS

1 large Aubergine

1 L cold Water

1 tsp Salt

2 small Red Onions

200g Cherry Tomatoes

1 Clove Garlic

1 tbsp Avocado Oil

1 tbsp Tomato Purée

1 tsp chopped Red Chili

½ tsp Paprika

½ tsp Turmeric

½ tsp Cumin

METHOD

Chop aubergine into small cubes. Soak them in the cold water and salt
Peel and chop the onions and garlic
Heat the avocado oil in a large wok style frying pan
Add the onions and garlic to the oil.
Rinse and drain the aubergine
Add this to the onions and garlic and fry on a low heat for 20 minutes,
Leaving the lid on, but remember to *stir* regularly
Chop the tomatoes.
Add the tomatoes, chili, spices and purée to the onion mix and cook for a further 20 minutes
If necessary, add a tablespoon of water during cooking

HUMMUS & TAHINI DIP

PREPARATION

Preparation: 10 minutes

Cooking Time: 0

Serves: 2

Oven: 0

NUTRITIONAL INFORMATION

TAHINI

Tahini is made from sesame seeds which is a good source of fibre and plant protein

TOP TIPS

You can make your own Tahini paste by blending sesame seeds with water and a sprinkling of salt.

I use tinned chickpeas as this makes it easier. You can also use the liquid from the tin to whisk up and use as an egg replacer for other recipes.

INGREDIENTS HUMMUS

250g Chickpeas (1 tin drained)
2 tbsp Hemp Oil
1 tsp (heaped) Tahini paste
1 Garlic clove
2 dsp cold Water
¼ tsp hot Paprika
¼ tsp Salt
½ tsp fresh Lemon juice

INGREDIENTS TAHINI

1 tsp (heaped) Tahini paste
25ml cold Water
Sprinkling of Paprika
Sprinkling of Hyssop
Splash of Hemp Oil
Sprinkling of Sesame seeds
3 Black Olives

METHOD

HUMMUS

Combine all the hummus ingredients in a blender, Blend until smooth
Spread the paste onto small round plates using the back of a spoon
Approximately 1cm deep. Leave a well in the middle

TAHINI

Place the Tahini in a small bowl
Slowly add the water a little at a time mixing thoroughly
Use the back of a spoon to make it easier
Continue adding water and mixing until it is smooth and light in colour and a runny consistency.
Pour the tahini into the well of the Hummus
Sprinkle with Paprika, Hyssop and Sesame seeds, Add Olives and a splash of oil over the top.

HEALTHY LENTIL SALAD

PREPARATION

Preparation: 10 minutes

Total Time: 10 minutes

Serves: 3

Oven: 0

NUTRITIONAL INFORMATION

GREEN LENTILS

Good source of protein, rich in iron and folate and low in calories.

TOP TIPS

I eat this on a detox day. When I have time I use dried lentils and beans rather than tinned. I soak them over night and then cook them for approximately 1 hour in water.

INGREDIENTS

1 tin of Black Beans

1 tin of Green Lentils

1 small Red Onion

2 Red Chili Peppers

1 Green Bell Pepper

Salt & Pepper to taste

METHOD

Drain and rinse the beans and lentils

Peel the onion and chop into small pieces

Chop the pepper and chili into small pieces

Mix all ingredients in a large bowl

Add salt and pepper to your required taste

MUSHROOM APPETISER

PREPARATION

Preparation: 10 minutes

Total Cooking Time: 13 minutes

Serves: 4 Sides

Oven: 0

NUTRITIONAL INFORMATION

MUSHROOMS

Contains vitamin B, C & D

TOP TIP

Best to eat straight away rather than reheating later as it becomes a little stodgy.

INGREDIENTS

500g Mushrooms

200ml Vegetable Stock

3 tbsp Gram Flour

2 tbsp Soy Sauce

2 tbsp Oil

2g grated Root Ginger

METHOD

Blend the stock, gram flour, soy sauce and ginger together in a small saucepan.

Heat and continuously stir for 3 minutes until it thickens

Then set aside.

Wash and slice the mushrooms

Heat the oil in a large pan

Cook the mushrooms in the oil with the lid on for 8 minutes

Add the sauce to the mushrooms and cook for a further 2 minutes

Great served with my rice & veg dish

NUTRITIOUS ORGANIC SALAD

PREPARATION

Preparation: 15 minutes

Cooking Time: 0 minutes

Serves: 2 mains or 4 sides

Oven: 0

NUTRITIONAL INFORMATION

VEGETABLES

Good source of Vitamins, Protein, fibre and antioxidants

TOP TIPS

I try to use organic ingredients where possible for most of my cooking

Don't leave the salad soaking in the dressing as it all goes soggy

INGREDIENTS

100g Sweetcorn kernels

50g Courgette strings

30g Carrot strings

10g Cress

50g Red Pepper

10 Cherry Tomatoes

1 small Avocado

80g Beetroot

130g Tofu

20g Spinach

10g Kale

15g crushed Walnuts

10g mixed Seeds

DRESSING

Juice of half a Lemon

1dsp Hemp Oil

1dsp Balsamic Vinegar

METHOD

Use a device to string the courgetti and carrot, if you don't have a device to do this, then shred or grate.

Chop the remaining vegetables and tofu into small pieces

Combine all main ingredients into a large bowl and mix

Prepare the dressing by combining lemon juice, oil and vinegar

Pour over the salad just before eating

POTATO PARCELS BOUREKAS

PREPARATION

Preparation: 20 minutes

Cooking Time: 45 minutes

Serves: 16 parcels

Oven: 210°C   20-25 minutes

NUTRITIONAL INFORMATION

POTATOES

High in carbohydrates

TOP TIPS

The stock I use is OSEM chicken flavor
It does not have any chicken in it.

You can freeze

INGREDIENTS

X2 packs of ready roll Puff Pastry (375g each)
700g peeled chopped Potatoes
1L Vegetable Stock
300g chopped Onions
½ tsp Turmeric
½ tsp Cumin
½ tsp Paprika
½ tsp Harissa
1 tbsp Rapeseed Oil
20ml Almond Milk plus a little to brush on top
Sesame Seeds to sprinkle on top

METHOD

Bring the stock to the boil in a medium saucepan
Add the potatoes, turmeric, cumin, paprika and harissa
Cook until tender, approximately 20 minutes
In the meantime, heat the oil and fry the chopped onions, 10 minutes
When cooked, drain the potatoes and mash them with the milk
Add the onions to the mashed potato and mix
Pre-heat the oven
Roll out the pastry, divide into 8 equal squares, 16 in total (2 sheets)
Place a small amount of potato mix on one half of the square, fold the other half over on top of it.
Seal the edges by pressing down with the back of a fork
Place on a baking sheet
Brush with milk and sprinkle with sesame seeds

Bake in the oven for 20-25 minutes

QUINOA SALAD

PREPARATION

Preparation: 10 minutes

Total Cooking Time: 10 minutes

Serves: 4

Oven: 0

NUTRITIONAL INFORMATION

QUINOA
High fibre content
Great super food and very nutritious

TOP TIPS

Make in the evening and leave in the fridge overnight, take to work in the morning.
Great nutritious and filling meal

INGREDIENTS

100g dried Quinoa

750ml Water

1 tin Chickpeas

1 tin Green Lentils

6 Cherry Tomatoes

3 Spring Onions

1 Celery stalk

50g baby Spinach

30g Cucumber

1 tsp fresh Lemon Juice

½ tsp Hemp Oil

Salt & Pepper to taste

METHOD

Heat the water in a saucepan and bring to the boil

Add the quinoa. Cook for 10 minutes, then raise and leave to cool

Drain and rinse the chickpeas and lentils

Finely chop all the other ingredients

Mix everything in a large bowl

Can be eaten warm or cold

SIMPLE SALAD
MIDDLE EASTERN STYLE

PREPARATION

Preparation: 10 minutes

Cooking Time: 0 minutes

Serves: 2 mains or 4 sides

Oven: 0

NUTRITIONAL INFORMATION

TOMATOES & CUCUMBER

High in nutrients & low in calories

TOP TIPS

Great served with pitta bread and my hummus dip
I always try to use Organic produce where possible.

INGREDIENTS

300g Tomatoes

200g Cucumber

50g Onions

1 Red Chili

2g fresh Coriander

1 tbsp Olive Oil

Juice of ½ a fresh Lemon

METHOD

Chop the tomatoes, cucumber, onion and chili into small cubes

Roughly chop the coriander

Combine all ingredients together and mix well

Serve

Mains

PREPARATION

Preparation: 10 minutes

Total Cooking Time: 50 minutes

Serves: 4

Oven: 20 minutes + 30 minutes 220°C

NUTRITIONAL INFORMATION

AUBERGINE

Good source of dietary fibre and low in calories

TOP TIP

Eat hot with a side order of roasted vegetables

STUFFED AUBERGINE

INGREDIENTS

2 large Aubergines
4 bell Peppers
½ Cauliflower
100g Mushrooms
1 tbsp Engevita Yeast Flakes
2 tbsp Oil
Salt & Black Pepper to taste

TOPPING
Grated Cheese (sprinkling)

METHOD

Wash the aubergines

Cut in half, length ways

Scoop out the spongy middle (this can be used in veg soup later)

Brush the aubergines lightly with oil

Place in oven for 20 minutes

Place cauliflower florets in a blender and zap until it resembles breadcrumbs

De-seed the peppers

Finely chop the mushrooms and peppers

Fry the peppers, mushrooms, cauliflower and yeast flakes in the oil for 10 minutes.

Spoon the mixture equally into the aubergines

Sprinkle with grated cheese on top

Bake for a further 30 minutes

CHICKPEA & SWEET POTATO BURGERS

PREPARATION

Preparation: 20 minutes

Total Cooking Time: 25 minutes

Serves: 6 – 8 Burgers

Oven: 0

NUTRITIONAL INFORMATION

CHICKPEAS

Good source of plant-based protein

TOP TIPS

Use some of the liquid from the chickpea tin to mix with the egg replacers. If you don't have any egg replacer you can whisk the chickpea liquid on its own.

Great served with caramelized onions, fries and salad

INGREDIENTS

0.5L Stock
400g tinned Chickpeas
1 large Sweet Potato
2 pressed Garlic cloves
40g ground mixed Nuts
50g Bread crumbs
75g Gram flour/Chickpea flour (Matzo meal can be used)
2 Egg replacers
4 sundried Tomatoes finely chopped
20g vegan cream Cheese
Oil for frying

METHOD

Peel and chop the sweet potato

Heat the stock

Cook the sweet potato, chickpeas and garlic in the stock, for

15 minutes (this is included in the preparations time)

Once cooked. Drain and place all ingredients in a large bowl

Mash together

Turn out onto a floured work surface

Divide into 6 to 8 equal pieces

Use your hands to shape as desired

Heat enough oil just to cover the bottom of a frying pan

Cook for approximately 10 minutes

BLACK BEAN CHILLI

PREPARATION

Preparation: 10 minutes

Cooking Time: 30-35 minutes

Serves: 4

Oven: 0

NUTRITIONAL INFORMATION

BLACKBEANS

Excellent source of nutrition, high in fibre, potassium, magnesium & protein

TOP TIPS

You can cook this in a slow cooker for the day and enjoy when you come home from work. In the slow cooker it absorbs the flavours even more, but you may need to add a little water.

INGREDIENTS

1 tin Black Beans (if you choose to use dried beans, then soak overnight & cook for 1-2 hours before hand or in the slow cooker all day.
1 tin chopped Tomatoes
2 medium size Onions
3 cloves of Garlic
1 Bell Pepper chopped
400g Vegan Mince
1 tsp mixed Herbs
1 tsp Cumin
1 tsp Chili Flakes
1 tbsp Oil
1 tbsp Tomato Purée
3 Vegetable Stock cubes (Kallø)
Salt and Pepper to taste

METHOD

Peel and chop the onions and garlic into small pieces

Heat the oil in a large pan

Fry the onions and garlic in the oil for 5 minutes

Add all the remaining ingredients and cook for 25-30 minutes or in a slow cooker all day if you prefer.

If using a slow cooker better to add a little water also.

Great served with a little grated cheese on top with Jacket Potatoes, Rice or even Pasta.

VEGAN MINCE CHILLI

PREPARATION

Preparation: 10 minutes

Total Cooking Time: 45 minutes

Serves: 4

Oven: 0

NUTRITIONAL INFORMATION

VEGAN MINCE
Good source of plant protein

TOP TIPS
This can be cooked as mentioned here, but you can also use a slow cooker and leave it all day to absorb all the flavours and tastes even better.

Great served on top of sweet jacket potatoes or with Jasmine rice and garlic bread

INGREDIENTS

1 pack of Naked Glory Vegan Mince
2 Red Onions
2 cloves of Garlic pressed
1 Red Bell Pepper
2 tins of chopped Tomatoes
1 tin of Red Kidney Beans
1 tin of Broad Beans
1tsp Cumin
1tsp Coriander
1tsp Chili Flakes
1tsp Paprika
1tsp Turmeric
1tbsp Tomato Purée
2tbsp Oil

METHOD

Peel, chop and fry the onions, garlic & bell pepper in 2 tablespoons of oil, in a large pan for 5 minutes.

Add all the remaining ingredients to the pan and stir.

Cook for 40 minutes with the lid on.

If you choose to cook in the slow cooker then add a little water as it will be cooking all day.

MOROCCAN STYLE COUS-COUS

PREPARATION

Preparation: 20 minutes

Total Cooking Time: 1 hour minimum

Serves: 6

Oven: 0

NUTRITIONAL INFORMATION

VEGETABLES

Packed with nutrients and vitamins

TOP TIPS

The longer its cooked the tastier it becomes. You can cook for an hour and leave it to rest and re-heat later, this has the same effect as it absorbs the flavours.

INGREDIENTS

STEW

2L Vegetable Stock

1 Courgette

1 Parsnip

1 Sweet Potato

1 Onion

2 Leeks

2 Carrots

2 Potatoes

2 cloves of Garlic crushed

½ an Aubergine

240g cooked Chickpeas (one tin)

(use the liquid from the chickpeas to mix with the flour)

½ red Pepper

½ green Pepper

3 dsp Gram Flour

1 dsp Corn Flour

2 dsp Tomato Purée

1 tbsp Rapeseed Oil

1 tsp of each, Turmeric, Cumin, Paprika and Harissa

COUS COUS

800g dried Cous Cous

600ml boiling Water

1tsp Stock powder

¼ tsp Black Pepper

METHOD

STEW

Heat the stew stock together with all the spices
Use the chickpea liquid to form a smooth paste with the gram flour, corn flour and tomato purée
Stir this into the stew stock
Top and tail the courgetti, aubergine, leeks, parsnip and carrots
Peel the garlic, sweet potato, onion and potatoes
Chop all the vegetables roughly
Add all vegetables to the stew stock
Cook for a minimum of 1 hour

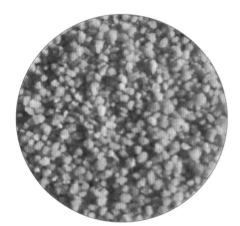

COUS COUS

Combine all the cous cous ingredients together in a large bowl
Soak for 5 minutes in the boiling water.
After soaking, use a fork to separate the cous cous granules making it light and airy, not all clogged together
Put the cous-cous in a steamer
Steam for 10-15 minutes before the stew is ready
Ideally steam above the soup stock

FALAFEL CHICKPEA BALLS

PREPARATION

Preparation: 10 minutes

Cooking Time: 10 minutes

Serves: 16 falafels

Oven: 0

NUTRITIONAL INFORMATION

CHICKPEAS
Good source of protein, dietary fibre and Iron.
No cholesterol

TOP TIPS

Falafel is great served with my homemade Hummus & Tahini dip, Mediterranean salad, Aubergine salsa, fries and pitta bread. Yummy

INGREDIENTS HUMMUS

250g Tin of Chickpeas
40g Bread
30g Gram Flour (chickpea flour) plus extra for rolling out
3 cloves of Garlic
50g Onion
1 Chili Pepper
15g dry Stock Powder
30ml Water
3g fresh Coriander
½ tsp Cumin
Black Pepper and Salt to taste if you wish
6 tbsp Oil for frying

METHOD

Peel the onion and garlic
With the exception of the flour for rolling and the oil for frying combine all the ingredients into a food processor, mix until everything is evenly mixed. If you have a good processor only takes 30-60 seconds.
Sprinkle the work surface with the extra gram flour.
Use your hands to make the mixture into small balls approximately 3cm in diameter.
Roll the balls on the floured surface, then set aside
Heat the oil in a large frying pan
If you have a deep fat fryer you can use that to cook them in.
Fry for 10 minutes until golden brown.

POTATO GNOCCHI

PREPARATION

Preparation: 20 minutes

Total Cooking Time: 30 minutes

Serves: 4

Oven: 0
Grill: 5 minutes

NUTRITIONAL INFORMATION

POTATOES

High in carbohydrates

TOP TIPS

Gnocchi is great with a side salad, it's surprisingly quite filling, so don't have big eyes and dish up too much

INGREDIENTS

GNOCCHI
330g Potatoes
330g Sweet Potatoes
2 L Vegetable Stock
20g vegan Parmesan
100g plain Flour

TOPPING
1 tbsp Tomato Purée
1 puréed Garlic
20g vegan Parmesan
Black Pepper to taste

METHOD

GNOCCHI

Peel and chop all the potatoes
Bring the stock to the boil and add the potatoes, simmer for 20 minutes
After 20 minutes, drain the potatoes but keep the stock for later
Place the potatoes, parmesan and flour in a bowl and mash.
Flour the work surface
Take a small amount of the mixture using a teaspoon and drop onto the floured work surface, shape into a gnocchi dumpling
Use the back of a fork to gently press the dumpling.
Bring the leftover stock to the boil again
Gently place the dumplings in the stock, cook for 3-4 minutes until they rise to the top, then drain well.

TOPPING

Place the tomato and garlic purée in a bowl and mix well
Add the dumplings and gently mix
Place in an oven proof dish
Sprinkle the parmesan over the top
Place under a hot grill for 5 minutes

VEGAN LASAGNE

PREPARATION

Preparation: 40 minutes

Cooking Time: 40 minutes

Serves: 6 mains

Oven: 200°C   40 minutes

NUTRITIONAL INFORMATION

VEGAN MINCE

Low in saturated fats and high in Protein

TOP TIPS

Great served with roast potatoes And salad

You can freeze it if you don't eat it all

22cm x 30cm dish used

INGREDIENTS

170g Carrots

150g Aubergine

150g Broccoli florets

150g red Onions

130g Mushrooms

200g fresh cherry Tomatoes

1 sweet Pepper

240g Vegan Mince

1 tin chopped Tomatoes

1L Stock

1tbsp Tomato Purée

2 cloves of Garlic

10 sliced black Olives

1tsp Basil Pesto

½ tsp dried mixed Herbs

½ tsp dried Nutmeg

5g fresh Rosemary

15g fresh Basil

1tbsp Rapeseed Oil

TOPPING

50g grated Cheese

100g white Block Cheese

1 jar of white vegan Sauce

LASAGNE SHEETS

9 sheets

METHOD

Chop carrots, broccoli and aubergine into small pieces, do not peel

Cook them in the stock for 10 minutes

Finely chop onions, pepper and garlic, Fry in the oil in a large wok style pan for 10 minutes

Drain the carrots, broccoli and aubergine
Halve the mushrooms

With the exception of the topping and lasagna sheets, combine all the remaining ingredients into the onion mixture.

Cook on a low heat with the lid on, for a further 10 minutes

Using a large oven proof dish 22cm x 30cm Place alternate layers of 3 lasagna sheets, layer of sliced block cheese, layer of
Main ingredients

Repeat this for 3 layers in total

Pour over the white lasagna sauce and sprinkle with the grated cheese

Bake in the oven for 40 minutes at 200°C

Divide into 6 equal portions and either serve or leave to cool and freeze

SPAGHETTI & SPICY MEATBALLS

PREPARATION

Preparation: 30 minutes

Total Cooking Time: 30 minutes

Serves: 4 people (20 meatballs)

Oven: 0

NUTRITIONAL INFORMATION

VEGAN MINCE

Low in saturated fats and high in Protein

TOP TIPS

Where possible use Naked Glory Mince. It's the best Vegan Mince on the market in my opinion.

INGREDIENTS

MEATBALLS

250g fresh Vegan Mince (or de-frosted)
2 Garlic cloves peeled
2 slices of dry Bread
50g mixed chopped Nuts
4 Egg Replacers (Orgran)
2 sprigs Fresh Thyme
2 sprigs Fresh Coriander
4 tsp Harissa (more if you like it hot)
Freshly ground Black Pepper
500g dry Spaghetti
750ml Boiling Water
 Grated Cheese for sprinkling on top

SAUCE

1 red Onion peeled
1 red Bell Pepper
1 green Bell Pepper
2 Chili Peppers
10 Cherry Tomatoes
2 tins chopped Tomatoes
1 tbsp Oil
1 tbsp Tomato Purée
1 tbsp Stock Powder
1 tbsp Balsamic Vinegar
1 tsp Brown Sugar

METHOD

MEATBALLS

Combine all the Meatball ingredients into a blender, combine well. Once blended, remove the mixture. Using your hands, form into small balls, approximately 3cm in diameter (ping pong size) set aside.

SAUCE

Peel the onions. Chop the onions, peppers and chilies very small
Heat the oil in a large pan
Fry the onions, peppers and chilies for 10 minutes on a low heat
Add the remaining sauce ingredients
Gently add the meatballs to the sauce and simmer for 20 minutes

SPAGHETTI

Cook the spaghetti in the boiling water for 10 minutes until tender
Drain the spaghetti
Share equally on your plate and place meatballs & sauce on top
Sprinkle with cheese if desired

CREAMY VEGETABLE MEDLEY

PREPARATION

Preparation: 10 minutes

Total Cooking Time: 40 minutes

Serves: 6

Oven: 20 minutes 200°C

NUTRITIONAL INFORMATION

VEGETABLES

Packed with many nutrients and health benefits

TOP TIP

This can be frozen for a later date, but freeze without baking in the oven. If you bake it and then freeze, it is quite dry when you re-cook it.

INGREDIENTS

Medley

8 small Potatoes
2 bell Peppers
1 Courgette
3 Leeks
2 large Carrots
½ a small Broccoli
½ a small Cauliflower
125g Spinach
1.75L Vegetable Stock
200g Mushrooms
2 Chili Peppers
1 tbsp Tomato Purée

Sauce

150g vegan Cream Cheese
400ml Cashew Milk
1 dsp English Mustard
2 tbsp Corn Flour

METHOD

Heat stock.

Wash vegetables

Roughly chop medley vegetables, leaving the chili's whole

Place all medley ingredients into the stock.

Cook for 20 minutes

Blend all the sauce ingredients together

Drain the vegetables and place in a large oven proof dish

Poor the sauce over the vegetables

Sprinkle with grated cheese on top

Bake for 20 minutes

MOUSSAKA

PREPARATION

Preparation: 30 minutes

Total Cooking Time: 1 hour

Serves: 4

Oven: 220°C 30 minutes

NUTRITIONAL INFORMATION

AUBERGINE

Good source of dietary fibre

TOP TIPS

Soak the slices of aubergine in salt water and lemon before frying as this can reduce the amount of oil they soak up.

INGREDIENTS

500g peeled Potatoes
½ L Vegetable Stock
800g Aubergine
2 medium Onions sliced
2 cloves Garlic sliced
4 large Tomatoes sliced
5 tbsp Oil
200g vegan Mince
200g cooked green Lentils
1 tsp Chili Flakes
100g vegan grated Cheese

METHOD

Cut the potatoes into 1cm thick slices
Bring the stock to the boil
Cook them in the stock until tender, approximately 15 minutes
Peel and slice the onions into rings
Peel and slice the garlic
Using only 1tbsp of the oil. Fry the onions and garlic for 5 minutes
Pre-heat the oven at this point
Slice the aubergine into ½ - 1cm slices.
Heat the oil and fry the aubergine slices in batches until soft
Drain the potatoes but keep the stock liquid
Combine the lentils, mince and chili with 3 tbsp of the stock liquid
Use a large oven proof dish. Place the ingredients in layers as follows
Potatoes, mince mixture, onions, aubergine, tomatoes, cheese
Finish with an extra layer of aubergine and cheese.
Bake for 30 minutes

MUSHROOM STACK

PREPARATION

Preparation: 20 minutes

Total Cooking Time: 1 hour

Serves: 4 Sides

Oven: 200°C

NUTRITIONAL INFORMATION

MUSHROOMS

Contains vitamin B, C & D

TOP TIP

Best served with a side salad

INGREDIENTS

4 large flat Mushrooms (Portobello)
400g Sweet Potatoes
250g red Onions
80g Spinach
1 large Bell Pepper
1 tbsp Oil
2 tsp Balsamic Vinegar
½ tsp Molasses (or brown sugar alternative)
Sprinkling of grated Vegan Cheese
(4 Chef's Rings)

METHOD

Heat the stock in a saucepan
Peel and chop the sweet potato into small pieces and place in the stock. Simmer for approximately 20 minutes until soft.
Remove the stalks of the mushrooms & place on a baking sheet
Slice the pepper into thin slithers
Heat the oil, fry the pepper on a low heat for 5 minutes then remove them from the pan and set aside.
Peel and slice the onions into rings. Use the same pan to fry the onions for 5 minutes, then add the balsamic vinegar & molasses for 5 minutes.
Drain and mash the potatoes. But keep the liquid.
Place the spinach in the drained liquid for 2 minutes until it wilts then thoroughly drain.
Using the chef rings, layer as follows: Potato, Onion, Pepper, Spinach, Potato, grated Cheese.
Gently place the rings on top of the mushrooms
Bake in a pre-heated oven for 20 minutes

MINI NUT LOAF

PREPARATION

Preparation: 15 minutes

Cooking Time: 25 minutes

Serves: 8 mini loaves

Oven: 200°C 25 minutes

NUTRITIONAL INFORMATION

NUTS

Nutrients, antioxidants and fibre
Anti-inflammatory properties
High in vitamin E

TOP TIPS

Mix the ingredients with your hands

I use mini loaf tins 9cm x 6cm

Egg replacer I use is Orgran

INGREDIENTS

300g roughly ground mixed Nuts

150g cream Cheese (violife creamy is good for this)

30g ground Flax Seed

75g Seeded Bread crumbs

2 tsp mixed Herbs

2 tbsp dry Stock Powder

1 tin Chick Peas

1 tsp English Mustard

2 Egg replacers

Oil for brushing

METHOD

Prepare the egg replacer by using 6 tbsp of liquid from the chickpea tin

Drain the remainder from the chickpeas and roughly mash them

Combine all ingredients into a large bowl

Mix well, I find this works best with your hands

Place greased parchment strips in each tin, this makes it easy to extract

Bake for 25 minutes

These can be cooled and frozen for another day

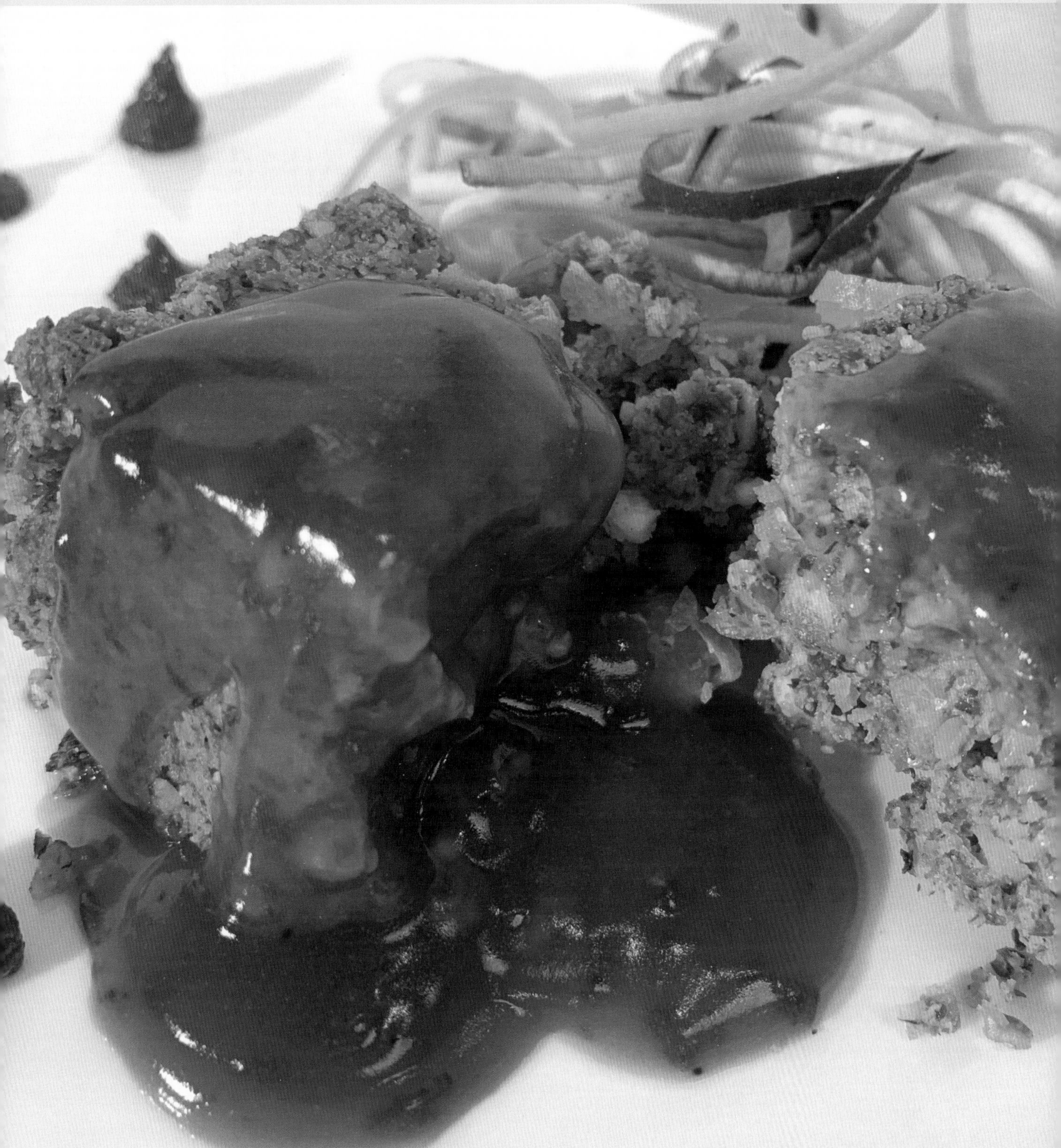

VEGAN MINCE PARCELS

PREPARATION

Preparation: 30 minutes

Total Time: 1 hour

Serves: 12 Parcels

Oven: 210°C 25 -30 minutes

NUTRITIONAL INFORMATION

VEGAN MINCE

Low in saturated fats and high in protein

TOP TIPS

Best eaten hot and fresh from the oven. Good with a side salad

INGREDIENTS

750g pre-made Vegan Puff Pastry (3 packets if bought)

200g Vegan Mince

1 Onion

1 large Potato

½ L Vegetable Stock

20g dried Cranberries

100g mixed Vegetables (tinned, frozen or fresh)

1 tbsp Oil

Salt & Pepper for taste

Non-Dairy Milk to brush pastry

Sesame Seeds to sprinkle before baking

METHOD

Peel and chop the onion and potato
Cook the potato in the stock for 20 minutes, then drain and mash
Fry the onion in the oil for 5 minutes
Mix all the ingredients together in a large bowl (not the pastry)
Pre-heat the oven at this point
Roll the pastry out on a floured worksurface and cut into your preferred shape, I do squares as they can be folded over to make triangles.
Place a spoonful of mixture on one side and fold the other side over to cover it.
Seal the edges with the back of a fork
Brush with non-dairy milk and sprinkle with seeds

DELICOUS NUTTY PARCEL

PREPARATION

Preparation: 40 minutes

Total Cooking Time: 40 minutes

Serves: 6

Oven: 180°C   30 minutes

NUTRITIONAL INFORMATION

NUTS
High in protein and potassium

TOP TIPS

This is one of my favorites
I make this into approximate size as follows: 30cm long x 10cm wide x 6cm high
You could make small individual ones if you prefer

INGREDIENTS

500g fresh Spinach
300g freshly ground mixed Nuts unsalted
3 large Red Peppers
400g Mushrooms
250g Greek White Block Cheese
100g grated hard Cheese
1 tbsp dry Stock Powder
4 tbsp Oil
½ tsp Nutmeg
12 sheets of Filo Pastry

METHOD

Cut the peppers into strips and de-seed them
Heat the oil in a large pan and fry the peppers until soft, 15 minutes
Remove from pan and drain, keep the remaining oil in the pan
Slice the mushrooms, then fry in the same pan with lid on for 5 minutes
In a separate bowl, combine the ground nuts, nutmeg, stock powder and grated cheese, mix well
Remove and drain the mushrooms, but leave the liquid in the pan
Mix the mushrooms into the ground nut mixture
Place the spinach in the remaining mushroom liquid, cook for 5 minutes
Until wilted. Then drain thoroughly.
Slice the white cheese into 2mm-3mm slices
Lay out a large sheet of foil and 3 sheets of Filo on top of the foil
Mold the foil into a loaf sharp. Lightly brush the filo with oil
Then start the layers, two layers of each.
Spinach, Peppers, white cheese, nut mix, and then repeat
Fold the filo over.
Lay out 3 more sheets of filo on the work surface and brush with oil.
Lay your parcel on top. Try to contain the shape. Wrap like a parcel
Do the same with the remaining filo. Sprinkle seeds on top if you wish
Bake in the oven for 30 minutes on the middle shelf

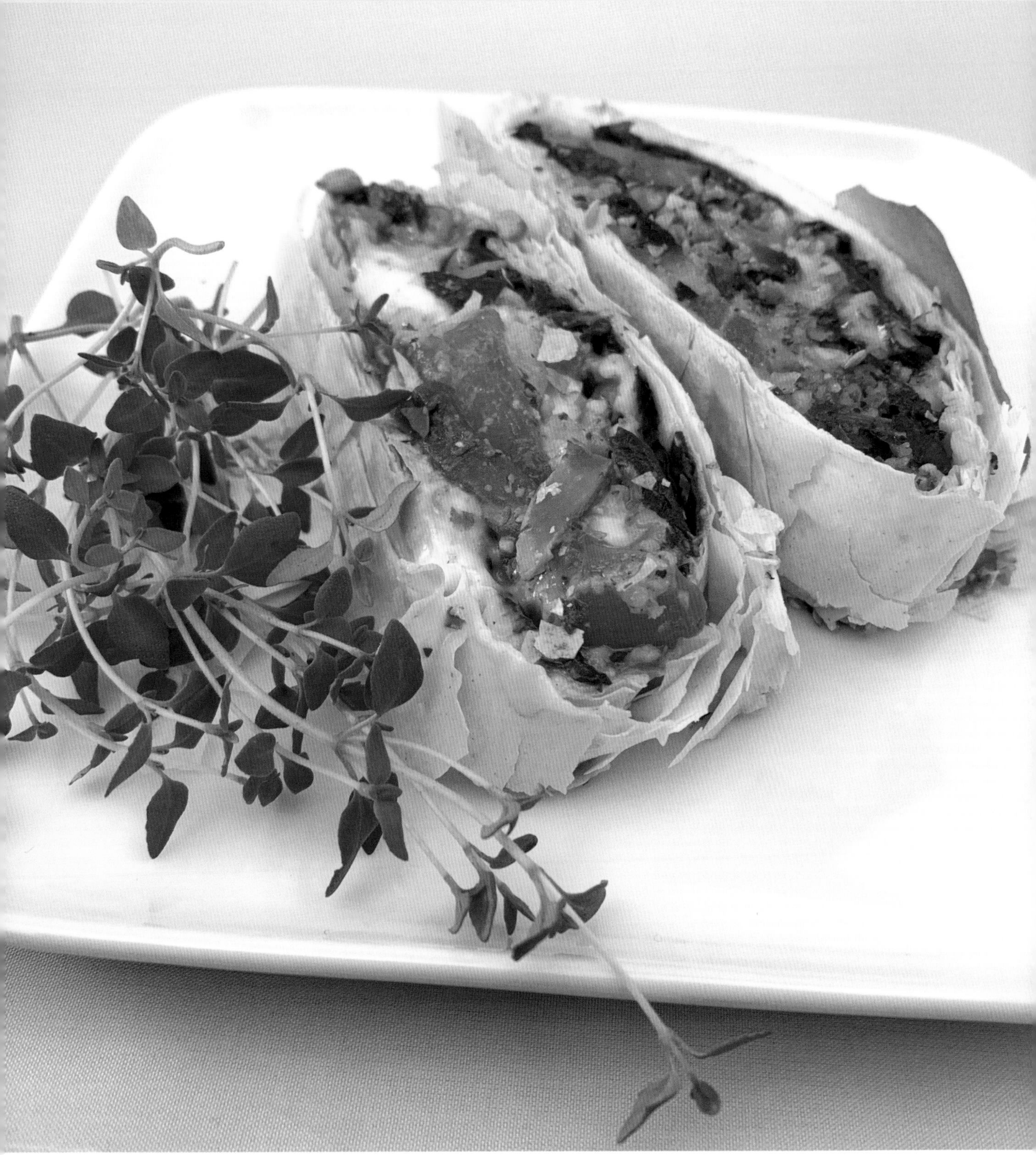

STEAMED PAK CHOI WITH TRIMMINGS

PREPARATION

Preparation: 30 minutes

Total Cooking Time: 30 minutes

Serves: 4

Oven: 0

NUTRITIONAL INFORMATION

PAK CHOI

Good source of many Vitamins, particularly Vitamin C, K and A

TOP TIPS

Nice served with Jasmine Rice

INGREDIENTS

2 Pak Choi sliced lengthways in half
4 fresh Mushrooms sliced
20g dried Porcini Mushrooms (soak in boiling water for 5 minutes)
½ Red Bell Pepper
½ Green Bell Pepper
2 Garlic Cloves pressed
1 pack of Tofu cut into strips
Juice of half Lemon
1tsp grated fresh Ginger
1tbsp Hemp Oil
1tbsp Soy Sauce
1tbsp Balsamic Vinegar

METHOD

Place the Pak Choi in a steamer for 30 minutes

Place the tofu, lemon, ginger, soy sauce & balsamic vinegar in a tub with a lid on and give it a gentle shake, so the tofu is covered.

Chop and de-seed the peppers into small pieces

Heat the oil in a large pan and add the peppers, fry for 5 minutes

Drain the porcini mushrooms.

Add all the mushrooms and garlic to the peppers, continue to cook on a low heat with the lid on for a further 5 minutes.

Add the mixture in the tub to the pepper mixture.

Cover and cook until the Bok Choy is done then serve.

MINCE & WILD MUSHROOM PIE

PREPARATION

Preparation: 20 minutes

Cooking Time: 30 minutes

Serves: 4 – 6 mains

Oven: 200°C 20-25 minutes

NUTRITIONAL INFORMATION

VEGAN MINCE

Low in saturated fats and high in Protein

TOP TIPS

Great served with roasted Vegetables

You can freeze if you don't eat it all

22cm x 30cm dish used

INGREDIENTS

320g Vegan Puff Pastry

1 large Red Onion

100g Wild Mushrooms

100g Open Mushrooms

450g Vegan Mince

750ml of thick Vegan Gravy

1 tbsp Oil for frying

1 tbsp Vegan Milk for brushing

METHOD

Pre-heat the oven to 200°C

Lightly brush a pie dish with oil

Peel, slice & fry the onion in the remaining oil until tender

Chop the mushrooms and add them to the onions

Add the mince and gravy, stir well

Pour into the pie dish

Roll out the pastry to the size required and place it on top of the mix

Brush the pastry with milk

Place in the oven for 20-25 minutes.

ARTICHOKE & OLIVE PIZZA TOPPING

PREPARATION

Preparation: 15 minutes

Total Cooking Time: 15 minutes

Serves: 1 medium pizza topping

Oven: 180°C for 15 minutes

NUTRITIONAL INFORMATION

ARTICHOKES

One of the most antioxidant rich vegetables. Low in fat and high in fibre and contains many vitamins

TOP TIPS

Use freshly made or pre-bought pizza base. See my recipe for homemade pizza base.

Great served hot, with cold salad.

INGREDIENTS

1 small Red Onion finely chopped

½ Red Bell Pepper

1 Artichoke heart cooked & chopped (ready bought in a jar can be used)

4 Garlic stuffed Olives sliced

4 button Mushrooms sliced

100g Greek White Block Cheese sliced (vegan goats' cheese)

1 tbsp Tomato Purée

1 tbsp vegan Pesto

1 tsp water

¼ tsp Chili Flakes if you like it spicy

METHOD

Brush the top of the pizza base with a thin layer of oil, this prevents the pizza from going soggy.

Mix the purée, pesto and water together (and chili flakes if you wish)

Spread this evenly over the pizza base

Lay the cheese on next

Then add the remaining ingredients on top of the cheese

Bake in the oven for 15 minutes

PIZZA BASE

PREPARATION

Preparation: 2 hours

Total Cooking Time: 6 minutes

Serves: 4 medium pizza bases

Oven: 160°C for 6 minutes

NUTRITIONAL INFORMATION

WHOLEWHEAT FLOUR

Good dietary fibre

TOP TIPS

Easier to use a bread maker

Roll out thinly as it will rise in the oven.

Either use fresh, or cool to freeze for another day.

INGREDIENTS

300ml Water

35ml Rapeseed Oil

250g Whole-wheat Flour

200g White Plain Flour

1 tsp Salt

1 tsp brown Sugar

1 tsp quick dried Yeast

METHOD

If you are doing this by hand, combine all ingredients and knead for 10 minutes. Place in a bowl, cover with a damp cloth and place in a warm area for 1 hour. Then follow the instructions from Knock back & knead.

I use a bread making machine to prepare the dough
Put the ingredients into the machine in the order stated
Set to a dough only setting, this takes approximately 1½ hours
Turn out onto a floured work surface
Knock back and knead
Divide into 4 equal pieces
Roll out to approximately ½cm in thickness
Bake in the oven for 6 minutes

GREEN QUICHE

PREPARATION

Preparation: 40 minutes

Cooking Time: 30 minutes

Serves: makes 3 Quiches

Oven: 180°C 20 minutes

NUTRITIONAL INFORMATION

GREENS

Packed with nutrients and vitamins

TOP TIPS

Use 15cm diameter pie dishes

If you use bought pastry, it's best to start making the contents first.

If you want to make the pastry yourself follow the Method

INGREDIENTS

BASE

200g plain Flour

1tsp Baking Powder

150ml Water

¼ tsp Hyssop

¼ tsp Stock Powder

1 dsp Hemp Oil

50g Margarine

X2 Egg replacers

Oil to brush

OR

400g bought Pastry

CONTENTS

1 small Onion sliced into rings

2 cloves of Garlic finely chopped

110g Broccoli florets

2 Leeks thinly sliced

½ Courgette cut into stringy spirals

100g vegan grated Cheese

125g Asparagus tips 5cm long

X6 Egg replacers
Handful of Spinach
½ L Stock
100g Crème Fraîche
1 tbsp Oil for frying

METHOD

BASE (HOME MADE)

Pre-heat the oven to 180°C
Combine all DRY ingredients into a large bowl
Rub in the margarine until it resembles breadcrumbs
Combine all the remaining base ingredients and bring together to form a dough
Roll out to 2-3mm on a lightly floured work surface
Place over a pie dish and trim the edges with a knife
Place in the oven for 10 minutes
Once removed from the oven, lightly brush with oil
Set aside

BASE (shop bought pastry)

Roll out on a lightly floured work surface
Place over a pie dish and trim the edges with a knife
Place in the oven for 10 minutes
Once removed from the oven, lightly brush with oil
Set aside

CONTENTS

Heat the oil
Use a frying pan to fry the onions, garlic and leeks for 5 minutes
Bring the stock to the boil in a saucepan
Boil the broccoli, courgette and asparagus for 3 minutes
I prefer to boil these separately as it just looks a mess if all together
Drain them but keep the stock
Use the remaining stock to wilt the spinach
Drain the spinach well by squeezing it with the back of a spoon
Mix ALL contents ingredients together in a bowl
Pour into the quiche base
Bake in the oven for 20 minutes

If you wish to freeze it, only bake for 10 minutes, then leave to cool before freezing

HOMEMADE SPINACH RAVIOLI

PREPARATION

Preparation: 30 minutes

Cooking Time: 12 minutes

Serves: 4

Oven: 0

NUTRITIONAL INFORMATION

SPINACH
High in Potassium and contains
Vitamin K & A

TOP TIPS

Use my homemade sauce.
If you have a Ravioli cutter it saves a
lot of time.

INGREDIENTS

PASTA

100g Spinach
200ml Vegetable Stock
200g Flour (I use Rye Flour)
5 heaped tsp Orgran Egg replacer

FILLING

1 Potato
100g Mushrooms
50g Vegan Halloumi
3 sprigs of fresh Basil

METHOD

PASTA

Heat the stock, add the spinach, cook for 2 minutes with lid on

Drain, Use 150ml of the stock liquid to mix with the egg replacer

Blend the spinach in a blender.

Using a large bowl, mix the flour, egg mixture & spinach together to form a dough.

Roll out to 1mm thick on a floured work surface

Add filling, fold over and seal into your desired shapes.

Cook in boiling water for 10 minutes

FILLING

Peel & chop the potatoes small.

Cook the potatoes for 10 minutes in boiling water, then drain.

Combine all filling ingredients in a blender for 30-60 seconds.

Place a teaspoon of mixture in each Ravioli and seal.

SPICY
RICE & LENTILS

PREPARATION

Preparation: 10 minutes
Plus 1 hour for soaking if you are using
dried lentils

Total Cooking Time: 1 hour

Serves: 4

Oven: 0

NUTRITIONAL INFORMATION

LENTILS

High in protein, fibre and iron

TOP TIPS

Make sure there is just enough liquid
not to dry up. When cooking is
finished it should have absorbed most
of the liquid, leaving the food moist.

INGREDIENTS

400g green Lentils

400g brown Rice

400g red Onions

1L Stock

2 tbsp Oil

1 tsp Harissa Paste

½ tsp Turmeric

½ tsp Cumin

METHOD

Combine the lentils, stock, harissa, turmeric and cumin in a saucepan
Bring to the boil
Simmer for 30 minutes with the lid on
Finely chop the onions
Heat the oil in a large pan
Fry the onions until soft, approximately 10 minutes
Drain the stock from the lentils, set it aside as this will be used later
Leave the lentils in the bottom of the saucepan
Place the onions on top of the lentils
Place the rice on top of the onions
Pour the remaining stock liquid on top of the rice, this should be just
enough to cover the rice. Make up a little more stock if necessary.
Simmer for a further 30 minutes with the lid on.
If you use white rice, less cooking is required

SPICY RICE & VEG

PREPARATION

Preparation: 10 minutes

Total Cooking Time: 35 minutes

Serves: 4

Oven: 0

NUTRITIONAL INFORMATION

BROWN RICE

High in fibre and low in cholesterol and fat

TOP TIPS

This dish is best to eat at the point of making it and not to reheat.

Great served with my Mushroom Appetiser.

INGREDIENTS

1 Onion

1 Bell Pepper

250g Brown Rice

100g Broccoli

100g Cauliflower

1 Courgette

800 ml Vegetable Stock

1 tbsp Oil

1 tsp Chili Flakes

½ tsp Turmeric

TOPPING

25g ground Almonds

25g Sultanas

METHOD

Chop the onion and pepper

Heat the oil in a large pan and fry the onion and pepper for 5 minutes

Add turmeric, chili flakes and rice

Stir for approximately 3 minutes, then move off from the heat

Wash and chop the vegetables in small pieces

Add the stock and vegetables to the rice

Return to the heat. Cook on a low heat for 25 minutes.

Sprinkle the almonds and sultanas over the rice mixture at the end and stir in for a further 2 minutes of cooking.

Serve hot.

VEGGIE-TOFU RICE

PREPARATION

Preparation: 15 minutes

Cooking Time: 25 minutes

Serves: 4

Oven: 0

NUTRITIONAL INFORMATION

VEGETABLES

Packed with various vitamins and minerals

TOFU
Good source of Protein

TOP TIPS

This can be adapted to whichever vegetables you have left over in the fridge.

INGREDIENTS

1 small Aubergine
2 Leeks
1 Celery stalk
1 small Carrot
1 small Courgette
1 Bell Pepper
1 Chili Pepper
3 Mushrooms
3 Broccoli florets
1 pack of Tofu (approximately 200-250g)
3 tbsp Oil
1 tbsp of powdered Stock

RICE
400g Brown Rice
1L Veg Stock liquid
Black pepper to taste

METHOD

Heat the stock in a saucepan and cook the rice for 25 minutes

Wash and chop all the vegetables into small pieces with the skin on

Chop the tofu into small pieces

Heat the oil in a large pan. Add all the vegetables & dry stock powder.

Fry for 15 minutes. Keep the lid on but stir regularly

Drain the rice

Add the rice to the vegetables and stir.

Serve straight away.

PUMPKIN & PEA RISOTTO

PREPARATION

Preparation: 15 minutes

Total Cooking Time: 1 hour

Serves: 4

Oven: 0

NUTRITIONAL INFORMATION

RISOTTO RICE

High in carbohydrates

TOP TIPS

When stirring, do this gently or it becomes a stodgy mess.

INGREDIENTS

450g Pumpkin (Squash can be used as an alternative)
½ bottle of white Wine
1 large red Onion
1 large red Pepper
250g frozen Peas
500g Risotto Rice
3 dsp Oil
1L Vegetable Stock
Black Pepper & Vegan Parmesan Cheese for sprinkling before eating

METHOD

Heat the stock in a large saucepan
Peel and chop the pumpkin into 1cm² (cubes)
Cook the pumpkin in the stock for 15 minutes
Add the peas to the stock and continue to cook for 5 further minutes
Peel the onion. Finely chop the onion and pepper
Heat the oil in a large wok style pan
Fry the onions and pepper in the oil. Low heat for 10 minutes
Remove from the pan and set aside
Rinse the rice.
Using the same pan as you used for the onions, fry the rice for 3 minutes
Add half of the wine to the rice and stir regularly
Drain the pumpkin and peas but keep the stock liquid
Continue to add the remainder of the wine to the rice to keep it moist
Use the remaining stock, if needed.
Add the pumpkin, peas, onions and pepper 5 minutes before the end
Cook the risotto for approximately 25 minutes in total

MEATY VEGAN SAUSAGES

PREPARATION

Preparation: 20 minutes

Cooking Time: 15 minutes

Serves: 15 Sausages

Oven: 0

NUTRITIONAL INFORMATION

NUTS

Nutrients, antioxidants and fibre
Anti-inflammatory properties and
High in Vitamin E

TOP TIPS

Great served with my sweet potato
Mash, fried onions and gravy

INGREDIENTS

1 medium Onion
2 cloves of Garlic
1 Celery stalk
100g mixed chopped Nuts
Handful of Kale
300g Tofu
55g grated Vegan Cheese
3 slices of dry seeded bread
1 chili Pepper
1 tbsp Tamari (soy sauce)
2 Egg replacers
1 tbsp Stock Powder
5 tbsp Oil for frying
Good sprinkling of Black Pepper
Gram Flour for rolling out

METHOD

Peel the onions & garlic

Chop the onions, garlic & chili. Fry in 2 tablespoons of oil

Combine all the OTHER ingredients into a food processor

Mix for approximately 1 minute until everything is combined nicely

Add the fried ingredients to the food processor

Mix for a further 20 seconds

Sprinkle a work surface with the gram flour

Roll out each sausage using your hands

Heat the remaining oil and fry the sausages for 15 minutes until
browned.

VEGAN SHAKSHUKA

PREPARATION

Preparation: 10 minutes

Cooking Time: minimum 30 minutes

Serves: 2 mains or 4 sides

Oven: 0

NUTRITIONAL INFORMATION

GARLIC

Little or no calories or fat in garlic
Some schools of thought say it may
Help to lower blood pressure and
cholesterol

TOP TIPS

Cook on a low heat for longer.
Sometimes I cook it for an hour.

Re-heat the next day and all the
flavours have absorbed and it tastes
even better.

Great with Hummus, Pitta & Fries

This can also be eaten cold as a salad

INGREDIENTS

1kg fresh Cherry Tomatoes

1 whole Garlic

2 large Sweet Peppers (any colour)

1 Chili Pepper or 1 tsp Harissa paste

1 tbsp Tomato Purée

1½ tbsp Rapeseed Oil

1 dsp Vegetable Stock Powder

½ tsp Turmeric

½ tsp Cumin

½ tsp Paprika

METHOD

De-seed the peppers and chili and thinly slice

Peel all the garlic cloves and cut each one in half

Heat the oil in a large pan or wok

Gentle fry the peppers, chili and garlic until tender

Cut the tomatoes in halves

Add all ingredients to the pepper mix

Cook on a low heat for 15 minutes with the lid on

Cook the last 15 minutes with the lid off, as this allows the excess juice

to evaporate.

SHEPHERDS PIE VEGAN STYLE

PREPARATION

Preparation: 35 minutes

Total Time: 1 hour

Serves: 6

Oven: 220°C 25 minutes

NUTRITIONAL INFORMATION

VEGAN MINCE

Good source of protein

TOP TIPS

Great served with gravy and roast vegetables.
I also like garlic bread with it.
You can freeze and eat another day

INGREDIENTS

FILLING

250g mixed chopped Vegetables
2 Onions
450g vegan Mince
2 cloves of Garlic
½ bottle of red Wine
100g purée Cashew Nuts
200g cooked green Lentils
100g chopped Tomatoes
1 tbsp Tomato Purée
1 tbsp Oil
Sprig of fresh Thyme
Black Pepper to taste

TOPPING

2 medium Potatoes
2 Sweet Potatoes
1 L Vegetable Stock
75g cream Cheese
30g grated Cheese for top

METHOD

TOPPING

Heat the stock.
Peel and chop all the potatoes and cook in stock for 30 minutes
When cooked, drain, but keep the stock liquid
Mash the potatoes with the cream cheese and set aside

FILLING

Peel and chop the onions and garlic and fry in the oil for 5 minutes
After the 5 minutes add all the remaining ingredients, mix gently
Also add 200ml of the left-over stock liquid (2 ladles)
Pour all the filling into an oven proof dish
Spread the mashed potato on top using a fork
Sprinkle with grated cheese and bake in the oven for 25 minutes

QUICK SPAGHETTI

PREPARATION

Preparation: 10 minutes

Cooking Time: 15 minutes

Serves: 2

Oven: 0

NUTRITIONAL INFORMATION

WHOLEMEAL SPAGHETTI

High in Carbs, contains Iron and protein. Low in fat and cholesterol

TOP TIPS

Best eaten straight away and not to reheat. Although you can eat it cold if you wish

INGREDIENTS

200g whole meal Spaghetti

1 L Vegetable Stock

¼ tsp Paprika

1 clove Garlic chopped very finely(you can use a garlic press)

8 Olives sliced

¼ green bell Pepper finely chopped

4 cherry Tomatoes quartered

1 tbsp Oil

METHOD

Heat the stock

Put the spaghetti in the stock

Simmer for 10 minutes, then drain.

In the meantime, prepare all the other ingredients

Add all the other ingredients to the spaghetti.

Cook on a low heat for a further 5 minutes and serve.

If you prefer, you can sprinkle vegan parmesan cheese on top

HAMIN (SLOW COOKED STEW)

PREPARATION

Preparation: 5 minutes

Cooking Time: 8 to 12 hours

Serves: 4

Oven: 0

NUTRITIONAL INFORMATION

CHICKPEAS

Good source of plant-based protein

TOP TIPS

Dried chickpeas can be used but must be soaked first and then rinsed. Any grains can be used for this dish. I prefer Quinoa and Pearl Barley

Great idea to prepare before work, switch on and let the slow cooker do the cooking for you, enjoy when you come home.

INGREDIENTS

1 tin of Chickpeas drained
4 large Potatoes
2 large Carrots
1 large Onion
4 cloves of Garlic
150g Pearl Barley, Split Peas, Bulgar Wheat, Grains, Quinoa
(Any of the above grains or pulses can be used, a mixture is good)
1.5 L Stock
1 heaped tsp Turmeric
1 heaped tsp Cumin
1 heaped tsp Paprika
1 tbsp Oil

METHOD

Wash the potatoes and carrots

Cut the ends off the carrots and then cut the carrots in halves

Peel and roughly chop the onion

Peel the garlic

Leave the potatoes whole

Combine all ingredients into a slow cooker

Leave on the low setting for 8 to 12 hours

Please read the instructions for your slow cooker for safety reasons

VEGAN MEATBALL STEW

PREPARATION

Preparation: 30 minutes

Total Cooking Time: 50 minutes

Serves: 6

Oven: 0

NUTRITIONAL INFORMATION

NUTS

Great source of many nutrients and high source of antioxidants

TOP TIPS

Great served with nice crusty bread

You can leave to cool and then freeze this for another day

INGREDIENTS

MEATBALLS

450g vegan Mince

2 cloves Garlic

100g mixed Nuts

3 slices stale Bread

6 Egg replacers (Orgran)

2 sprigs of fresh Thyme

2 sprigs of fresh Coriander

1tsp Harissa

Black pepper for taste

Oil for frying

STEW

1.3kg Potatoes

600g Peas

300g Onions

1.6L Stock

1tsp Turmeric heaped

1tsp Cumin heaped

1tsp Paprika heaped

1tbsp Oil

METHOD

STEW

Peel and chop the potatoes and onions

Combine all the stew ingredients and cook for 50 minutes

MEATBALLS

Peel the garlic

Combine the garlic, bread, nuts, thyme and coriander in a blender

Once blended, combine all the meatball ingredients into a large bowl and bring together with your hands.

Form into small meatballs

Heat a shallow amount of oil in a frying pan and fry until browned

This will seal the meatballs

Gentle place the meatballs into the stew for the remainder of the 50 minutes.

MUSHROOM STROGANOFF

PREPARATION

Preparation: 15 minutes

Cooking Time: minimum 1 hour
Or all day in a slow cooker

Serves: 4 mains

Oven: 0

NUTRITIONAL INFORMATION

MUSHROOMS

High in antioxidants, Selenium and
Vitamin D

TOP TIPS

Even tastier if you leave all day in the
slow cooker

INGREDIENTS

650g chopped Mushrooms

10 cloves of Garlic

250g Onions

2 bell Peppers sliced

200ml vegan Crème Fraiche

500ml Ale

200ml plain vegan Yoghurt

3 tbsp Gram Flour

1 heaped tbsp Stock powder

1 tbsp Avocado Oil

½ tsp Chili Flakes

METHOD

Peel, chop and fry the onions and garlic in the avocado oil

Approximately 10 minutes until soft

Combine ALL ingredients in a large saucepan on the hob

OR in the slow cooker.

Great served with Jasmine rice

CHEESY OPEN TART

PREPARATION

Preparation: 15 minutes

Total Time: 45 minutes

Serves: 4

Oven: 200°C 30 minutes total

NUTRITIONAL INFORMATION

TOMATOES

Good source of a number of vitamins and good source of antioxidant Lycopene.

TOP TIPS

Best eaten hot and fresh from the oven. Good with a side salad

INGREDIENTS

1 roll Vegan Pastry (shop bought)

2 medium sized Onions

150g Cherry Tomatoes

1 tbsp Balsamic Vinegar

1 tsp brown Sugar

1 tbsp Oil

Fresh Basil

200g vegan Greek white Cheese

METHOD

Heat the oven to 200°C

Peel and slice the onions thinly.

Heat the oil and gently fry the onions for 5 minutes, add the balsamic vinegar and sugar to the onions and continue cooking for 3 minutes

Unroll the pastry, leave it on its grease proof paper and place in oven

Bake for 10 minutes until slightly browned and puffed up

Remove from the oven and flip the pastry over, return to oven for a further 5 minutes. Then remove and set aside.

Using a pizza cutter or knife, cut the pastry into 4 equal pieces

Evenly spread the onion mix over the pastry

Roughly chop the basil and sprinkle on top of the onions

Thinly slice the cheese and lay on top of the basil

Cut the tomatoes in halves and evenly place on top.

Bake in the oven for 10 to 15 minutes

Desserts

BREAD & BUTTER PUDDING

PREPARATION

Preparation: 10 minutes

Cooking Time: 20 minutes

Serves: 4

Oven: 180°C   20 minutes

NUTRITIONAL INFORMATION

SULTANAS

Good source of antioxidants
Fibre & Potassium

TOP TIPS

Best eaten hot.
Great old English traditional dessert
Based on my Mum's original recipe

INGREDIENTS

4 slices of Whole meal Bread (you can use gluten free if you wish)

50g vegan hard block Butter

50g Brown Sugar

50g Sultanas (or dried fruit of your choice)

TOPPING

300ml dairy free Milk

X4 equivalent Egg Replacers (I use Orgran)

½ tsp Cinnamon

METHOD

Pre-heat the oven

Grease a 1.5L oven proof dish

Generously butter each slice of bread

Cut the bread to the shape of your dish

Place the first layer of bread & butter in the bottom of the dish

Sprinkle with half the sugar and half the sultanas

Place a second layer of bread & butter on top

Sprinkle the remaining sugar and sultanas on top

Using a separate bowl, mix the milk, eggs and cinnamon together

Pour the liquid over the bread layers

Bake for 20 minutes

CHOCOLATE BUTTON BUNS

PREPARATION

Preparation: 10 minutes

Cooking Time: 30 minutes

Serves: 12 Buns

Oven: 190°C   30 minutes

NUTRITIONAL INFORMATION

MILK CHOCOLATE BUTTONS

No essential Nutrients unfortunately but they taste great.

TOP TIPS

Leave to cool for about 15 minutes after cooking and eat warm as the chocolate is still soft and melted. Don't eat straight from the oven as the chocolate could scold you.

INGREDIENTS

120g dairy free Margarine

200g Caster Sugar (you can use coconut sugar)

170g Plain Yoghurt (I use Alpro)

300g Plain Flour sieved

125g Vegan Chocolate Buttons

2 Egg equivalents (Orgran egg replacer is good)

1 tsp Baking Powder

1 tsp White Wine Vinegar (Cider Vinegar can be used)

1 tsp Vanilla Essence

METHOD

Pre-heat the oven to 190°C

With the exception of the chocolate buttons, place all the ingredients into a large mixing bowl.

Use an electric mixer to mix the ingredients thoroughly

Stir the chocolate buttons in using a spoon.

Spoon the mixture into the bun cases

Bake on the middle shelf (in a fan oven) or top shelf in a conventional

CHOCOLATE CHIP COOKIES

PREPARATION

Preparation: 5 minutes

Cooking Time: 20 minutes

Serves: 12

Oven: 180°C   20 minutes

NUTRITIONAL INFORMATION

DARK CHOCOLATE

Good source of Antioxidants but sugars contain on essential nutrients

TOP TIPS

Great to eat warm as they are crispy on the outside and soft inside, just like cookies should be.

INGREDIENTS

230g dairy free Margarine

150g Demerara Sugar

270g Plain Flour sieved

100g Dark Chocolate Chips or Raw Cacao nibs

1 tsp Baking Powder

1 tsp Vanilla Essence

2 tbsp Almond Milk

½ tsp Cider Vinegar

METHOD

Pre-heat the oven to 180°C

With exceptions of the chocolate chips, Place all ingredients in a large bowl. Mix well, with a spoon or a hand blender

Add the chocolate chips and mix in with a spoon.

Lightly grease and lightly flour a large flat baking sheet

Place a spoonful of the mixture at even spaces on the baking sheet

Place in the oven for 15 to 20 minutes

Cut into the shapes you desire after they are baked

CHOCOLATE & COCONUT MOUSSE

PREPARATION

Preparation: 3 minutes

Cooking Time: 10 minutes on hob

Serves: 8 small pots

Oven: 0

NUTRITIONAL INFORMATION

DARK CHOCOLATE

If you use good quality dark chocolate with a high cocoa content then it is packed with antioxidants. However, do remember chocolate has a high calorie count.

TOP TIPS

I use 100% dark chocolate, it's very bitter. If you use this then use one tablespoon of icing sugar, but if you use vegan milk chocolate then you won't need to use any icing sugar.

INGREDIENTS

350g Coconut Collaborative

50g dairy free Chocolate

1 tbsp Icing Sugar (if needed, see tips)

METHOD

Break the chocolate into piece

Place in an oven proof bowl

Place the bowl above a saucepan of boiling water

It's best to use a bowl bigger than the saucepan

Stir the chocolate until its melted, approximately 10 minutes

Remove from the heat

Stir the coconut collaborative into the chocolate

Mix thoroughly

Spoon into small pots

Leave to cool

Then pop in the fridge

CHOCOLATE ORANGE CAKE

PREPARATION

Preparation: 15 minutes

Cooking Time: 40 minutes

Serves: 16 squares

Oven: 180°C   40 minutes

NUTRITIONAL INFORMATION

DARK CHOCOLATE

Good source of antioxidants

But sugars contain No essential Nutrients

TOP TIPS

Allow to cool after cooking and then you can freeze the squares individually and take them out when needed.

If you then want to eat them hot, microwave from frozen for 40 seconds

Great with ice cream

INGREDIENTS

300g Demerara Sugar

100g Dark Chocolate

400g self-raising Flour

200ml Rapeseed Oil

430ml Water

2 tbsp grated Orange rind

3 tbsp squeezed Orange juice

2 tsp Baking Powder

½ tsp Cider Vinegar

Pinch of Salt

METHOD

Pre-heat the oven to 180°C

Lightly grease a large oven proof dish approximately 22cm x 30cm

Melt the chocolate in a suitable bowl over boiling water

Combine all ingredients in a large mixing bowl and blend thoroughly

Pour into the greased dish

Place in the centre of the oven for 40 minutes

CHOCOLATE ORANGE COOKIES

PREPARATION

Preparation: 10 minutes

Cooking Time: 20 minutes

Serves: 12

Oven: 180°C   20 minutes

NUTRITIONAL INFORMATION

DARK CHOCOLATE

Good source of Antioxidants but sugars contain on essential nutrients

TOP TIPS

Great to eat warm as they are crispy on the outside and soft inside, just like cookies should be.

INGREDIENTS

100g dairy free Margarine

100g Caster Sugar

100g Plain Flour sieved

65g Dark Chocolate

50g Desiccated Coconut

1 Egg replacer (Orgran egg replacer is good)

1 tsp Baking Powder

Zest of one Orange

Juice of one Orange

METHOD

Pre-heat the oven to 180°C

Using a large bowl, beat the sugar & margarine together until creamy.

Add all the remaining ingredients and mix well.

Grease a baking tray.

Pour the mixture onto the tray and spread out evenly.

Bake for 20 minutes

Remove from the oven and cut into your desired shapes.

PREPARATION

Preparation: 20 minutes + 10 in freezer

Cooking Time: 15 minutes

Serves: 20 large or 40 small

Oven: 180°C   15 minutes

NUTRITIONAL INFORMATION

COCONUT

No Cholesterol in Coconuts
Rich in dietary fibre
High in saturated fat

TOP TIPS

Vegan butter works much better than margarine for this recipe
You can also use fresh grated coconut if you wish

COCONUT COOKIES

INGREDIENTS

100g Demerara Sugar

200g Margarine or Vegan Butter

100g Desiccated Coconut

250g Self Raising Flour

3 tbsp freshly squeezed Orange Juice

½ tsp Vanilla Essence

Pinch of Salt

60g Dark Chocolate (optional)

METHOD

With the exception of the chocolate, place all other ingredients into a large mixing bowl.

Mix well, either by hand or electric mixer

Wrap the mixture in clingfilm and place in the freezer for 10 minutes

Pre-heat the oven

Lightly flour a work surface

Take the mixture from the freezer and gently roll out to 5mm thickness

Cut into preferred shapes

Place on a lightly grease baking sheet

Bake in the oven for 15 minutes in a fan oven or slightly longer in other

Optional – once cooked, melt chocolate and dip the edges in.

DATE FILLED COOKIES

PREPARATION

Preparation: 40 minutes + 2 hours in the fridge

Total Cooking Time: 20 minutes

Serves: 40 cookies

Oven: 180°C   10 minutes per batch

NUTRITIONAL INFORMATION

DATES

High in fibre and antioxidants

TOP TIPS

When placing the filling on the pastry, dip your fingertips in cold water so the jam doesn't stick to your fingers.
I use 6cm diameter cookie cutter but you can use any size.
These are my favorite cookies

INGREDIENTS

PASTRY

500g plain Flour
150g Sugar
150g vegan Butter
Finely grated rind of 3 Oranges
Juice of 1 to 2 Oranges
½ tsp Vanilla essence

FILLING

150g chopped Dates
2 tbsp Plum Jam
2 tbsp Cocoa powder

METHOD

PASTRY

The pastry is best made using a food processor
Mix all dry ingredients together
Chop the butter into small piece and add gradually to the dry mix on the pulse setting, until it resembles breadcrumbs.
Add the orange rind and vanilla extract
Gradually add the orange juice until it all comes together to form a dough.
Place the dough in cling film and put in the fridge for minimum 2 hours

FILLING

Blend all filling ingredients in the food processor, blend until smooth.
Pre-heat the oven
Flour a work surface
Roll out the pastry to approximately 3mm thick
Cut into circles and place a small amount of filling in the middle.
Dab the edges with water and fold up the sides to form a triangle.
Place the scraps back in the fridge, keep cold at all times.
Place on the top shelf in a fan oven for 10 minutes.
Upon removal from the oven, sprinkle with icing sugar.

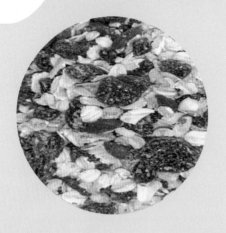

HOMEMADE CEREAL

PREPARATION

Preparation: 10 minutes

Total Cooking Time: 0

Serves: 10 breakfasts

Oven: 0

NUTRITIONAL INFORMATION

SEEDS & NUTS

Rich in protein, magnesium, potassium
Plant iron, calcium and vitamins

TOP TIPS

Store in a sealed container and use all week.
I eat mine with fresh sliced oranges but you can eat with yoghurt or milk

I use organic products where possible

INGREDIENTS

400g Oats

250g Bran

300g mixed Sultanas/Raisins

100g milled Flaxseed

100g mixed Seeds

100g Cranberries

150g mixed ground Nuts

50g Goji Berries

30g dried Chia Seeds

METHOD

Combine all ingredients in a large bowl

Mix well

I use 2 metal spoons, one in each hand to mix

HOMEMADE PROTEIN SNACKS

PREPARATION

Preparation: 20 minutes

Cooking Time: 5 minutes

Serves: 18 Squares

Oven: 0

NUTRITIONAL INFORMATION

NUTS

Nutrients, antioxidants and fibre
Anti-inflammatory properties and
High in Vitamin E

TOP TIPS

I wrap them individually and put them
in the freezer. Take one out each
morning for my lunch box.

INGREDIENTS

40g Porridge Oats (I use gluten free Organic)
30g Oat Bran
20g mixed Seeds
30g mixed Nuts
10g Goji Berries
10g Chia Seeds
20g ground Flax Seeds
150g pitted chopped dates
40g dark Chocolate (this is optional)
1 tbsp pure Maple Syrup

METHOD

Place the mixed seeds, nuts and goji berries in a blender with a metal
blade. Three quick pulses with the blender will be enough
With the exception of the chocolate,
Combine all ingredients in a large bowl, mix together with your hands
Melt the chocolate in a large suitable bowl, over boiling water
Once melted, add all the ingredients to the chocolate and mix well.
Lay out on parchment paper and shape by hand
Approximately 1-2cm thick
Cut into your desired shapes with a small pastry cutter.
Leave to cool and harden.

LEMON CHEESECAKE

PREPARATION

Preparation: 15 minutes

Cooking Time: 1 minute

Serves: 8 small pots

Oven: 0

NUTRITIONAL INFORMATION

LEMONS

Good source of Vitamin C

TOP TIPS

Ideal to double bag the biscuits before crushing, or you could have a mess all over the kitchen.

INGREDIENTS

100g Chocolate Biscuits (I use bourbon but check first, as they are not all vegan)

100g Plain Biscuits (I use rich tea, but again not all makes are vegan)

300g Creamy Cheese (Violife is good for this)

½ tin a Coconut Milk (just the thick creamy part not the watery milk)

½ tsp Vanilla Essence

1tbsp Vegan Butter

1tbsp Icing Sugar

Juice of ½ a Lemon

METHOD

Place all the biscuits in a sealed bag

Using a rolling pin or something similar, Crush the biscuits

Melt the butter in a saucepan, then remove from the heat and mix the biscuits into the melted butter.

Equally share the biscuit mix between your pots and compact lightly.

Combine all the remaining ingredients into a blender, blend well.

Equally share the cheese mix between your biscuit pots

Place in the fridge

LIME CHEESECAKE

PREPARATION

Preparation: 10 minutes

Cooking Time: 2 minutes

Serves: 4

Oven: 0

NUTRITIONAL INFORMATION

LIMES

Good source of Vitamin C

TOP TIPS

Most Bourbon biscuits are vegan Or if you prefer plain then you could use Rich tea

A chef's ring is ideal to use for your Cheesecakes but don't worry if you don't have these, any little pot will be sufficient.

INGREDIENTS

80g vegan Biscuits of your choice

1dsp Coconut Oil

160g Coconut Collaborative

70g vegan Cream Cheese

30g plain Alpro yoghurt

2 heaped tsp Icing Sugar

2 Limes grated zest

1 Lime Juice

METHOD

Place the biscuits in a sealed bag and hammer with a rolling pin until crushed into crumbs.

Melt the coconut oil in a saucepan for 2 minutes

Remove from the heat and mix the crumbs into the oil

Divide the mixture equally and place in the bottom of your pots

Compact down

Combine all the remaining ingredients together and mix well

You can now either spoon your mixture onto the biscuit base or pipe it in, either way works.

Sprinkle a little zest on top if you desire

Place in the fridge until you are ready to eat.

STRAWBERRY CHEESE CAKE

PREPARATION

Preparation: 15 minutes

Cooking Time: 1-2 minute
1 hour in fridge

Serves: 8 small pots

Oven: 0

NUTRITIONAL INFORMATION

STRAWBERRIES

Good source of Vitamin C & Folate B9

TOP TIPS

Double bag the biscuits before crushing as the bag may split and crumbs will be everywhere.

INGREDIENTS

100g Chocolate Biscuits (Bourbon)

100g plain Biscuits (Rich tea)

300g thick Creamy Cheese (Violife is good for this)

200g Strawberries

½ can of the condensed Coconut Milk (not the watery part)

½ tsp Vanilla Essence

1 tbsp vegan Butter

1 tbsp Coconut Oil

1 tbsp Icing Sugar

METHOD

Crush the biscuits in a sealed bag using a rolling pin

Melt the butter in a small saucepan

Remove from the heat and mix in the crushed biscuits

Equally share the biscuit mix between the pots and compact lightly

Combine the cream cheese, coconut milk, vanilla essence, coconut oil and icing sugar in a blender. Blend well

Place the cheese mix in the pots on top of the biscuits equally

Blend the strawberries and place on top of the cheese

Place in the fridge for 1 hour minimum

RHUBARB CRUMBLE PIE

PREPARATION

Preparation: 30 minutes

Total Cooking Time: 35 minutes

Serves: 1 large Pie

Oven: 200°C   25 minutes total

NUTRITIONAL INFORMATION

RHUBARB

Contains Fibre, Vitamin C, K & B Complex and potassium

TOP TIPS
Great served hot with ice cream and the remaining juice

INGREDIENTS

FILLING
12 Organic Rhubarb stalks (ideally from your garden)
80g Sugar
½L Water
BASE
200g Plain Flour
100g Vegan Margarine or Butter
50ml Ice Cold Water
Pinch of Salt
TOPPING
150g Plain Flour
75g Vegan Margarine or Butter
50g mixed Ground Nuts
75g Sugar
½ tsp Cinnamon

METHOD

Pre-heat the oven to 200°C.
FILLING Chop the rhubarb into 5cm lengths
Use a saucepan, cook them for 10 minutes in the water and sugar
Then drain, but keep the juice as you may like to use that later.

BASE Combine the flour and margarine. Use your fingertips to make it resemble breadcrumbs. Slowly add the water, mixing with a knife, bring together and place in cling film. Pop in the fridge for 15 minutes. Then roll the pastry out on a floured work surface, to the size of your large flan case. Trim the edges off and bake for 10 minutes in the oven. Remove from the oven and place your rhubarb filling in the flan.

TOPPING Combine all topping ingredients into a large bowl and fluff into breadcrumbs as before. Spread evenly over the top of the pie. Bake for a further 15 minutes

BASIC SPONGE CAKE

PREPARATION

Preparation: 10 minutes

Cooking Time: 20 minutes

Serves: 16 squares

Oven: 200°C   20 minutes

NUTRITIONAL INFORMATION

Not a whole lot of goodness in this but it does taste good.

TOP TIPS

This cake is really good as the base to my Milky Cake or even a base for trifle.

INGREDIENTS

200g Caster Sugar

200g Self-raising Flour

200g Margarine

1 tsp Vanilla Essence

1tbsp Lime or Lemon Juice

8 Egg Replacers

METHOD

Pre-heat the oven to 200°C

Prepare an oven proof dish approximately 20x30cm

Place the sugar and margarine in a large mixing bowl

Beat until smooth and creamy

Add all remaining ingredients and mix well, by hand or mixer

Pour into the oven proof dish

Bake at the top of a fan oven for 20 minutes

MILKY CAKE

PREPARATION

Preparation: 10 minutes

Cooking Time: 5 minutes

Serves: 16

Oven: 0

NUTRITIONAL INFORMATION

Not a whole lot of goodness in this but it does taste good.

TOP TIPS

Leave to set in the fridge before serving

INGREDIENTS

1 Basic Sponge Cake (see recipe)

200g Caster Sugar

1 tbsp Vanilla Essence

4 Egg Replacers

1 tbsp powdered Vegan Gelatin

50ml Milk non-dairy

350g Coconut Collaborate cream

Chopped Nuts and grated Chocolate for sprinkling on top at the end

METHOD

Mix the gelatin, milk, vanilla essence and sugar in a saucepan

Heat for 3 minutes until the sugar dissolves continuously stirring

Add the remaining ingredients and stir for a further 2 minutes until

smooth and creamy.

Pour the mixture evenly over the sponge base and place in the fridge

until cool.

VEGAN TIRAMISU

PREPARATION

Preparation: 15 minutes

Cooking Time: 0

Serves: 4 small pots

Oven: 0

NUTRITIONAL INFORMATION

DARK CHOCOLATE

Good source of antioxidants

But sugars contain No essential Nutrients

TOP TIPS

Best to pop in the fridge after you have made them.

INGREDIENTS

¼ cup of strong good quality Coffee

1 tsp of Sugar (add this to the coffee)

40g dark Chocolate grated

1 tbsp soft white vegan cream Cheese

3 tbsp Coconut Collaborative

½ tsp Vanilla Essence

1 tsp Icing sugar (or you can use Maple syrup)

4 Sponge fingers (see my recipe or buy a plain sponge and cut it up)

METHOD

Make the coffee, add the sugar and leave to cool

Combine the cream cheese, coconut collaborative, vanilla essence and icing sugar in a bowl. Mix well

Cut the sponge to the size of your little pots

Dip each sponge very quickly into coffee, don't allow it to go soggy

Place the sponge in the bottom of the pot

Sprinkle with grated chocolate

Pipe or spoon a layer of cheese mixture on top

Then repeat with a second layer of each

Sprinkle the remaining chocolate on top if you wish

Drinks, Smoothies Miscellaneous

BLACKBERRY SMOOTHIE

PREPARATION

Preparation: 3 minutes

Cooking Time: 0

Serves: 2

Oven: 0

NUTRITIONAL INFORMATION

BLACKBERRIES

Contains many essential nutrients also high in Vitamin C, K & A

TOP TIPS

Best to drink it straight away. Great way to start the day
Blackberries can be picked wild though August/September but do wash them before using.

INGREDIENTS

100g Blackberries

Handful of Spinach

750ml Coconut Milk

1 Apple (remove the core)

METHOD

Place all ingredients into a blender

Blend for 1 minute

Drink and enjoy

BLUEBERRY SMOOTHIE

PREPARATION

Preparation: 3 minutes

Cooking Time: 0

Serves: 2

Oven: 0

NUTRITIONAL INFORMATION

BLUEBERRIES

Contains many essential nutrients also high in Vitamin C

TOP TIPS

Best to drink it straight away. Great way to start the day

INGREDIENTS

10 Blueberries

5 Grapes

Small handful of Kale

400ml Almond Milk or Hazelnut Milk

2 Almonds

METHOD

Place all ingredients into a blender

Blend for 1 minute

Drink and enjoy

DETOX DRINK

PREPARATION

Preparation: 5 minutes

Cooking Time: 0

Serves: 2

Oven: 0

NUTRITIONAL INFORMATION

BEETROOT
Good source of Vitamin B9 & C and good source of fibre, potassium and iron

TOP TIPS

Best to drink it straight away. Great way to start a healthy day

INGREDIENTS

35g beetroot (from a jar or home cooked)

1 Carrot

1 Orange

10g Kale

1 cup of Green or White Tea (not English tea but proper White Tea)

Juice of ¼ Lemon

Thin slice of Ginger

METHOD

Rinse the beetroot

Use cold green/white tea

Top and tail the carrot (cut the ends off) then roughly chop.

Peel the orange and check there are no pips in it

Place all ingredients into a blender

Blend for 1 minute

Drink and enjoy

ENERGY SMOOTHIE

PREPARATION

Preparation: 5 minutes

Cooking Time: 0

Serves: 2

Oven: 0

NUTRITIONAL INFORMATION

Nuts

Good source of dietary fibre and contain a wide range of essential nutrients

TOP TIPS

Great start to the day to boost your energy levels

INGREDIENTS

½ a small Pineapple

1 Apple (core removed)

½ a Banana

250ml Coconut Milk

1 tsp ground Flax seed

1 tsp Hemp seeds

¼ tsp Chia seeds

2 Almonds

2 Hazel Nuts

2 Walnuts

1 Brazil Nut

METHOD

Combine all ingredients into a blender

Blend on full speed for 1 minute

Serve

GREEN TEA & PINEAPPLE DRINK

PREPARATION

Preparation: 5 minutes

Cooking Time: 0

Serves: 2

Oven: 0

NUTRITIONAL INFORMATION

GREEN TEA

Packed with Antioxidants

TOP TIPS

Best to drink it straight away. Great way to start the day

INGREDIENTS

½L Cold Green Tea
½ a peeled Pineapple
10 mixed Nuts
Juice of half a Lemon

METHOD

Place all ingredients into a blender
Blend for 1 minute then stop and blend for a further 1 minute
Drink and enjoy

HAZELNUT MILK SMOOTHIE

PREPARATION

Preparation: 5 minutes

Cooking Time: 0

Serves: 2

Oven: 0

NUTRITIONAL INFORMATION

HAZELNUT MILK

Rich in Vitamin B's and E
Best to use unsweetened
I use Organic if possible

TOP TIPS

Best to drink it straight away. Great
way to start the day

INGREDIENTS

750ml Hazelnut Milk
1 Banana peeled
Handful of Spinach
½ an Avocado peeled
½ a Papaya peeled

METHOD

Place all ingredients into a blender
Blend for 1 minute
Drink and enjoy

CARAMELISED ONIONS

PREPARATION

Preparation: 5 minutes

Cooking Time: 15 minutes

Serves: 4

Oven: 0

NUTRITIONAL INFORMATION

RED ONIONS

Good source of Antioxidants from Vitamin C, B6 and B9

TOP TIPS

Goes really well with my homemade burgers or my sausage & mash

INGREDIENTS

3 large Onions

1 tbsp Oil (I like to use Organic Rapeseed Oil)

1 tbsp Balsamic Vinegar

1 tsp Molasses

METHOD

Top and tail the onions and remove the outer skin.

Thinly slice the onions into rings

Heat the oil in a large pan

Add the onions, set on a low heat with the lid on for 10 minutes

After 10 minutes add the balsamic vinegar & molasses for 5 minutes.

HOMEMADE PASTA SAUCE

PREPARATION

Preparation: 5 minutes

Total Cooking Time: 20 minutes

Serves: 4

Oven: 0

NUTRITIONAL INFORMATION

TOMATOES

Packed with Vitamins, A, B6, C, E and K

TOP TIP

If I have lots of time, I prefer to use fresh tomatoes and peppers but otherwise this is very quick and easy.

INGREDIENTS

1 jar of Roasted Red Peppers (you can roast them yourself if you wish)

2 tins of chopped Tomatoes (you can use fresh if you wish)

2 Red Onions

1 tbsp Oil

1 tsp Harissa

1 tsp Lemon Juice

1 Garlic clove

½ tsp Mustard

½ tsp Salt

METHOD

Peel and chop the onions into small pieces

Heat the oil in a pan.

Fry the onions for 10 minutes on low heat with the lid on

Combine all the other ingredients in a blender and zap until smooth

Pour the smooth mixture into the fried onions and heat for 10 minutes

Ready to serve with your pasta of choice

QUICK
PASTA SAUCE

PREPARATION

Preparation: 5 minutes

Total Cooking Time: 10 minutes

Serves: 4

Oven: 0

NUTRITIONAL INFORMATION

TOMATOES

Packed with Vitamins, A, B6, C, E and K

TOP TIP

If I have lots of time, I prefer to use fresh roasted peppers but otherwise this is very quick and easy.

INGREDIENTS

1 jar of Roasted Red Peppers

160g fresh Tomatoes

2 cloves of Garlic

3 sprigs of fresh Basil

1 tbsp Tomato Purée

½ tsp Sugar

1 tsp Balsamic Vinegar

3 Mushrooms

METHOD

Combine all ingredients into a blender

Blend for 1 minute

Heat in a pan for 10 minutes

Serve on top of your pasta

SWEET POTATO MASH

PREPARATION

Preparation: 10 minutes

Cooking Time: 30 minutes

Serves: 4

Oven: 0

NUTRITIONAL INFORMATION

SWEET POTATOES

Rich in antioxidants and high in fibre and beta carotene

REGULAR POTATOES

Mainly consists of carbohydrates

TOP TIPS

Great served with my Meaty Vegan Sausages, fried onions and gravy

INGREDIENTS

3 medium sized Sweet Potatoes

3 medium sized regular Potatoes

1L Stock

100ml dairy free Milk

Black Pepper to taste

METHOD

Peel and chop all the potatoes

Bring the stock to the boil

Add the chopped potatoes to the boiling stock

Simmer for 30 minutes

Drain the potatoes

Add the black pepper and milk

Mash well and serve

GRANARY ROLLS

PREPARATION

Preparation: 2 hours

Cooking Time: 25 minutes

Serves: 12 Rolls

Oven: 200°C   25 minutes

NUTRITIONAL INFORMATION

SEEDS

Good source of protein, iron and polyunsaturated fats

TOP TIPS

Great with homemade soup

INGREDIENTS

450g Granary Flour

270ml Water

5ml non-dairy Milk

1tsp Salt

2tsp Molasses

1½ tsp dried Yeast

Non-dairy Milk to brush over the rolls before baking

Mixed Seeds to sprinkle over the rolls before baking

METHOD

Combine the ingredients in a bowl and mix well

Knead well on a floured work surface for approximately 5 minutes

Place in a bowl and cover with greased clingfilm

Leave in a warm place for 1 hour

Turn on to a floured work surface and knock back (knead lightly)

Cut into 12 equal pieces

Place on a lightly greased baking tray and cover with greased clingfilm

Leave in a warm place for a further 50 minutes until doubled in size

Brush with milk and sprinkle generously with seeds

Bake in the oven for 25 minutes

OLIVE
FLAT BREAD

PREPARATION

Preparation: 1 hour 30 minutes

Cooking Time: 20 minutes

Serves: 3 medium flat breads

Oven: 210°C

NUTRITIONAL INFORMATION

OLIVES

Olives do contain fat but it's the Healthy kind, Monounsaturated. They are also rich in Vitamin E

TOP TIPS

If you have a bread maker it's much easier to use this to mix and prove the dough.

If you use butter, melt it first, if you use margarine, no need to melt.

INGREDIENTS

450g plain Flour

12 black Olives sliced

1 tsp dried Yeast

2 tsp Sugar

1 tsp Salt

300ml warm Water

70g vegan Butter or Margarine

1 tsp dried Hyssop

TOPPING

Oil to brush

Poppy seeds or Sesame

Chili Flakes

METHOD

Combine all the main ingredients in a bowl or bread maker
If you do this by hand, turn out onto a floured work surface and knead for a good 10 minutes. If using a bread maker, it will do it for you.
Place it in a clean bowl and cover with cling film or damp cloth
Leave to rise in a warm place for 1 hour to prove
Pre-heat the oven to 210°C
After the dough has been left to rise, place on a floured work surface
Knock back by kneading again, add more flour as needed
Divide into 3 equal pieces
Flatten out with your hands into the shape that you desire
Place on a baking sheet and lightly brush with oil
Sprinkle on your topping of seeds or chili flakes or both
Place in the oven for 20 minutes.